# *READ TO WORK*

# SERVICE & RETAIL

## LINDA STERN

**CAMBRIDGE ADULT EDUCATION**
A Division of Simon & Schuster
Upper Saddle River, New Jersey

*Author:* **Linda Stern**

*Series Editorial Consultant:* Harriet Diamond, *President, Diamond Associates, Multifaceted Training and Development, Westfield NJ*

*Reviewers:*
Margaret Kirkpatrick, *Berkeley Adult School, Berkeley CA*
Jackie Anger, *Institute for Labor Studies and Research, Cranston RI*

*Director, Editorial & Marketing, Adult Education:* Diane Galen
*Market Manager:* Will Jarred
*Assistant Market Manager:* Donna Frasco
*Editorial Development:* Learning Unlimited, Inc.
*Project Editors:* Douglas Falk, Elena Petron
*Editorial Assistant:* Kathleen Kennedy
*Production Director:* Kurt Scherwatzky
*Production Editor:* John Roberts
*Art Direction:* Pat Smythe, Kenny Beck
*Cover Art:* Jim Finlayson
*Interior Design & Electronic Page Production:* Levavi & Levavi
*Photo Research:* Jenifer Hixson

Printed in the United States of America
  3 4 5 6 7 8 9 10      01  00

ISBN: 0-8359-4685-1

**CAMBRIDGE ADULT EDUCATION**
A Division of Simon & Schuster
Upper Saddle River, New Jersey

# CONTENTS

To the Learner      v

## UNIT 1    TRAVEL AND RECREATION JOBS      1

**Lesson 1**

**Guiding Tourists and Visitors**      2
> READING SKILL: FINDING THE MAIN IDEA
>> READINGS: Convention Guide, Flier, Employee Handbook

**Lesson 2**

**Driving a Taxicab or Car for Hire**      8
> READING SKILL: FINDING SUPPORTING DETAILS
>> READINGS: Newspaper Ad, License Examination, Guidelines for Drivers

**Lesson 3**

**Driving Passengers on a Bus**      16
> READING SKILL: MAKING INFERENCES
>> READINGS: Employee Manual, Note and Map, Bus Schedule

**Lesson 4**

**Selling Tickets**      24
> READING SKILL: UNDERSTANDING VISUAL INFORMATION
>> READINGS: Team Schedule, Seating Map, Price Chart

**Unit Review**      30

## UNIT 2    JOBS WORKING WITH CHILDREN      31

**Lesson 5**

**Providing Child-Care Services**      32
> READING SKILL: FOLLOWING DIRECTIONS
>> READINGS: Directions, Trip Instructions, Family Day-Care Handbook

**Lesson 6**

**Helping in the Classroom**      40
> READING SKILL: FOLLOWING DIRECTIONS
>> READINGS: Conference Schedule, Class Schedule, Training Schedule

**Lesson 7**

**Coaching and Counseling Children**      46
> READING SKILL: DISTINGUISHING FACT FROM OPINION
>> READINGS: Notice to Counselors, Evaluation Report, Day Camp Handbook

**Unit Review**      54

## UNIT 3   HOTEL AND RESTAURANT JOBS                                55

### Lesson 8
### Preparing Foods                                                  56
READING SKILL   CLASSIFYING INFORMATION
READINGS:  Chart of Baked Goods Orders, Inventory List, Menu Chart

### Lesson 9
### Taking Care of Guests                                            64
READING SKILL:  COMPARING AND CONTRASTING
READINGS:  Brochure, Business Letter, Price List

### Lesson 10
### Working At A Cash Register                                       72
READING SKILL:  DISTINGUISHING FACT FROM OPINION
READINGS:  Diagram, Making Change Guidelines, Memo

### Lesson 11
### Serving Food                                                     78
READING SKILL:  IDENTIFYING CAUSE AND EFFECT
READINGS:  Safety Tips, Setup Procedures, Machine Instructions

### Unit Review                                                      84

## UNIT 4   RETAIL SALES JOBS                                        85

### Lesson 12
### Working as a Salesperson                                         86
READING SKILL:  DRAWING CONCLUSIONS
READINGS:  Memo, Magazine Article, Training Program Information

### Lesson 13
### Working as a Salesclerk                                          94
READING SKILL:  DRAWING CONCLUSIONS
READINGS:  Cash Register Receipt, Sales Receipt, Refund Slip

### Lesson 14
### Working as a Stock Clerk                                         100
READING SKILL:  UNDERSTANDING VISUAL INFORMATION
READINGS:  BAR GRAPH, FLOW CHART, FLOOR PLAN

### Unit Review                                                      106

### Respelling Guide                                                 107
### Resources                                                        108
### Glossary                                                         110
### Index                                                            113
### Answer Key                                                       114

# TO THE LEARNER

Welcome to the *Read To Work* series. The books in this series were written with you, the adult learner, in mind. Good reading skills are important in the world of work for these reasons:

- ◆ They may help you get the job you want.
- ◆ They will help you learn how to do your job well.
- ◆ They can help you get a better job.

The lessons in this book, *Read To Work: Service and Retail,* will help you improve your reading skills. As you work through the lessons, you will also learn about jobs in different service businesses and in retail sales.

## UNITS

*Read To Work: Service and Retail* is divided into four units. Each unit covers different kinds of jobs. You can look at the **Contents** to see what fields and jobs are covered in this book.

## LESSONS

Each unit contains at least 3 lessons. Each lesson teaches one reading skill and covers one kind of job. Here are some things to look for as you read each lesson:

**Words to Know** are words you will learn in the lessons. Look for the meaning of each new word to the left of what you are reading. You will also see a respelling of the words like this: *pronunciation* (proh-nun-see-AY-shuhn). This respelling will help you say the word correctly. There is a guide to help you with the respellings on page 107.

**Job Focus** describes the job in the lesson. It also tells you what types of skills are needed to do the job.

**How It Works** teaches you about the reading skill and how you can use it.

**Readings** include memos, pages from handbooks and manuals, posters, product guidelines, safety notices, and articles from company newsletters. If you look through this book, you will see that the reading passages look different from the rest of the lesson. They are examples of reading materials from the world of work.

**Check Your Understanding** questions can be multiple choice, short answer, or true/false. They will help you check that you understand the reading.

**On the Job** gives you a chance to read about real people as they do their jobs.

## OTHER LEARNING AIDS

There are other learning aids at the back of the book. They are:

**Respelling Guide:** help with pronouncing words
**Resources:** where to get more information on the jobs in the book
**Glossary:** definitions of the Words to Know
**Index:** job names in the book
**Answer Key:** answers to *Check Your Understanding* and *Lesson Wrap-Up* questions

Now you are ready to begin using *Read To Work: Service and Retail.* We hope that you will enjoy this book and learn from it.

# Unit One

# • Travel and • Recreation Jobs

Bus drivers and taxicab drivers are two travel workers described in this unit. They transport people to work, school, and other important places. Tourist guides and ticket sellers work in recreation jobs. They help provide people with information and entertainment choices.

People who work in travel and recreation need good reading skills on the job. In this unit, you will learn about some of the reading materials that are used in these jobs. These reading materials include guide books, maps, and price charts. All these materials give workers information that helps them do a better job.

This unit teaches the following reading skills:

◆ finding the main idea
◆ finding details that support the main idea
◆ making inferences
◆ understanding visual information

You will learn how workers in travel and recreation use these reading skills in their work.

# Guiding Tourists and Visitors

**▼▼▼▼▼▼▼▼▼▼▼**

### Words to Know

annual

brochures

clients

convention

employee

flier

professional

reservation

tourist

When traveling to a place you don't know well, you may need help planning your trip. You may need help choosing a place to stay. You may need ideas about good places to eat. Or you may need help when planning to do some sight-seeing.

A tourist guide can help with these needs. Tourist guides work in hotels, convention centers, and travel agencies. They might even work for government tourist offices.

In many places, tourism is big business. Tourists and business people need information in order to plan their travel. They need information about cities, resort areas, hotel rooms, restaurants, and meeting places.

Tourist guides gather information. They read material to get the exact information that a tourist or visitor needs. Tourist guides need to be good at **finding the main idea** of their reading material. This is important because it helps them answer questions from tourists.

## Job Focus

**Tourist guides** need to have good reading skills. They must be able to read schedules, maps, and charts. They must be able to read different kinds of short booklets. They must also use directories like the telephone *Yellow Pages* to find information.

Tourist guides may work at a convention center information booth, or a desk in a hotel lobby. Because they work in crowded places, tourist guides may have to help many people at once. They must be polite and friendly. They must speak clearly because some foreign visitors may not understand English well.

Opportunities for tourist guides can be found in cities, resort areas, theme parks, and historic places.

# Finding the Main Idea: How It Works

Every paragraph has a main idea. The main idea is the most important idea of the paragraph. **Finding the main idea** means figuring out the most important point that the writer states. This skill helps you understand the meaning of what you read.

Read the introduction to the convention guide below.

annual (AN-yoo-ehl) yearly; every year

convention (kuhn-VEHN-shun) a general meeting of members of a group

professional (proh-FEHSH-uhn-uhl) very skilled or highly trained

## CONVENTION GUIDE

**W**elcome to our 25th **annual convention!** As you know, three days of **professional** workshops and sessions lie ahead. When you're not at convention events, however, take the time to get to know our wonderful host city—New Orleans. This guide has been put together especially for you and your family. The goal is to help you enjoy your stay in this beautiful city. Here you will find listed many of the exciting points of interest that have made "the birthplace of jazz" famous worldwide.

What is the topic of the paragraph? To find the topic ask yourself, "What is this paragraph about?" Think of words that describe the topic of the paragraph. We can say that the topic is *getting to know New Orleans*.

What is the main idea of the paragraph?

_____

_____

Ask yourself, "What does the writer want me to know about this topic?" Does the writer want to remind you about workshops? Yes, but that is not the main idea. Think about words and phrases like *guide, goal, enjoy, wonderful host city,* and *exciting points of interest*.

You could say that the main idea is *this guide was put together to help people enjoy New Orleans*. Sometimes, the main idea of a paragraph is not stated in one sentence.

Hint: Writers often, but not always, state the main idea in the first or last sentence of a paragraph.

**flier** (FLEYE-uhr) a printed sheet of paper, usually folded, which contains information

**tourist** (TOOR-ihst) someone who is traveling, often for sight-seeing

The following **flier** is one of many that a tourist guide might read to gather information. A well-informed tourist guide can offer a **tourist** more choices and better service.

Read the following flier. Then, answer the questions that follow.

---

# BRIGHT LIGHTS, CITY SIGHTS

For almost 20 years, BRIGHT LIGHTS, CITY SIGHTS TOURS has been showing the exciting sights of New York City to tourists from here and abroad. Let us show you the New York you've always dreamed about. Join us for the Harbor Tour, the Downtown Tour, or the Sights of Manhattan Tour—or all three!

Our Harbor Tour takes you to all of New York's dramatic harbor sights. You'll sail down the East River past the South Street Seaport. Next, you'll circle the beloved Statue of Liberty. Finally, it's on to Ellis Island, home to the Ellis Island Immigration Museum.

Historic Greenwich Village, including Washington Square Park and Bleecker Street, is the first stop on the Downtown Tour. Next, you'll visit art galleries in Soho and then stop for coffee and pastries in Little Italy. The tour ends with a walk down Chinatown's famous Mott Street.

On our Sights of Manhattan Tour, you'll visit such well-known spots as the Empire State Building, which stands one-quarter mile high. You'll also see the United Nations building, Rockefeller Center, and Lincoln Center for the Performing Arts.

---

## CHECK YOUR UNDERSTANDING

Answer each question based on the flier above.
1. What is the main idea of the first paragraph?

    a. Bright Lights, City Sights has been in business for almost 20 years.

    b. For exciting sight-seeing tours of New York City, use Bright Lights, City Sights.

    c. Bright Lights, City Sights can show you all the places that you've dreamed about.

**LESSON 1 ◆ GUIDING TOURISTS AND VISITORS**

**2.** What is the main idea of the second paragraph?

    a. Ellis Island is a point of interest on the Harbor Tour.
    b. The Harbor Tour is a tour of New York's harbor sights.
    c. There is a lot to learn about the waterways.

**3.** What is the main idea of the third paragraph?

    a. The Downtown Tour explores places to eat.
    b. The Downtown Tour shows more sights than the other tours.
    c. The Downtown Tour explores different cultural and ethnic areas.

**4.** What is the main idea of the fourth paragraph?

    a. The Empire State Building is one-quarter mile high.
    b. The Sights of Manhattan Tour includes well-known tourist spots.
    c. On this tour, you see mostly buildings.

*Check your answers on page 114.*

## ON THE JOB

Alice opened a box of fliers. She pulled out some of the fliers and put them on a nearby rack. Then, she opened her calendar of events. Now, she was ready for business.

Alice works as a tourist guide at a busy convention center. On this day more than 3,000 members of a teacher's group were there for a yearly convention.

Convention goers ask Alice when they need information about the city. She can find points of interest on maps. She will look up restaurant telephone numbers for reservations. She even arranges for theater tickets for convention goers.

Alice enjoys looking up information. But most of all, Alice loves showing off her hometown to visitors.

### TALK ABOUT IT

**1.** Describe three things that Alice does on the job.

**2.** Discuss the kinds of materials Alice reads for her job.

**employee** (ehm-ploi-EE) a person hired by another to work for wages or salary

**reservation** (rehz-er-VAY-shuhn) a promise to hold a space

**brochures** (broh-SHORZ) small booklets of information

**clients** (KLY-ehnts) customers

Some tourist offices give their workers an **employee** handbook. Handbooks often give information about what is expected of employees on the job.

○ **YOUR JOB IS IMPORTANT!**

Our guests come from all over the world. They are here to enjoy themselves. It is a tourist guide's job to help them experience the special attractions of this great city.

It is important to give guests complete information. For example, suppose a guest asks for a **reservation** for ○ a bus tour. Make sure to give the exact location, starting time, number of hours, and fee.

How you look is very important. Your clothes should always be neat and clean. The information booth should be orderly. Fliers and **brochures** should be easy to reach.

Equally important is your attitude. Remember the three **P**'s—Be **p**leasant, **p**olite, and **p**rompt when you answer **clients**. Your helpful attitude will encourage ○ guests to return.

## CHECK YOUR UNDERSTANDING

Answer each question based on the reading above.

1. What is the main idea of the first paragraph?

    a. Guests come from all over the world.
    b. Guests are here to enjoy themselves.
    c. A tourist guide helps guests enjoy a city's attractions.

2. What is the main idea of the second paragraph?

    a. A tourist guide needs to be an expert.
    b. It is important to give complete information for every request.
    c. Always give the location, number of hours, and fee for a tour.

3. What is the main idea of the third paragraph?

    a. An employee's appearance and workplace should be neat and orderly.
    b. An employee's clothes should always be neat and clean.
    c. Guests should be able to get fliers and brochures.

**4.** The *topic* of the fourth paragraph is

    a. getting guests to return.
    b. having a good attitude.
    c. answering clients.

**5.** What is the main idea of the fourth paragraph?

    a. It's important to remember clients.
    b. A good attitude will encourage guests to return.
    c. Answer client requests pleasantly, politely, and promptly.

*Check your answers on page 114.*

## ◆ LESSON WRAP-UP

Every paragraph has a main idea. The main idea is based on the topic. The main idea makes an important point that the writer wants you to know about the topic.

To find the main idea of a paragraph, ask yourself, "What important thing does the writer want me to know about the topic?" Look for important ideas in the first and last sentences.

Read the topics below. Write a main idea that could be the focus of a discussion or paragraph. Use complete sentences.

**Example:** Topic: Airport safety

**Main Idea:** Even though it may take more time and money, extra security at airports is important.

**1.** Topic: Supermarket prices

Main Idea:

**2.** Topic: Crime prevention

Main Idea:

**3.** Topic: Violence on television

Main Idea:

*Check your answers on page 114.*

# L e s s o n  2

## Driving a Taxicab or Car for Hire

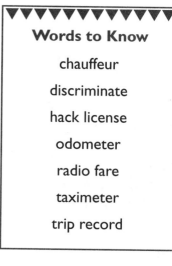

**▼▼▼▼▼▼▼▼▼▼▼**

**Words to Know**

chauffeur

discriminate

hack license

odometer

radio fare

taximeter

trip record

In many towns, people can hire a car to drive them places. People use this service when they don't have their own car. Or they may not want to leave their car somewhere like the airport.

The hired car may be owned by a car service or by a taxicab company. People telephone and arrange for a hired car to pick them up. People may also hail, or signal for, a taxicab on the street.

A driver's main goal is to get riders where they want to go, both safely and quickly. To do so, a driver must choose the best route. Weather and traffic should be considered. Finding out these details helps the driver meet the goal of a quick, safe trip.

A writer uses details to make the main point of a paragraph or story clearer. **Finding supporting details** in a paragraph helps the reader understand the writer's meaning.

## Job Focus

**Hired car drivers** and **taxi drivers** need a regular driver's license (LEYE-suhns) and a taxi driver's license. A license is a legal permit. To get a taxi driver's license, they may have to pass a written test or go through a training program.

Drivers must know the local driving laws and the taxicab rules. They need to know the area, how to read maps and street signs, and how to follow directions.

Taxi drivers may have to pass an exam in English listening skills. Drivers also should be patient and polite to passengers.

Jobs for drivers of taxis and hired cars are expected to increase faster than most jobs through the year 2005.

# Finding Supporting Details: How It Works

Main ideas and supporting details go together. Supporting details are statements that tell more about the main idea. With facts and examples, they tell what the main idea means. Details explain things such as *who*, *when*, *where*, or *how*.

**Finding supporting details** will help you understand main ideas. The details make the main idea clearer.

Read the newspaper ad below.

---

## DRIVERS WANTED

The Greenwood Car Service is looking for highly skilled drivers. You must have a clean driving record and a valid **hack license.** You must have at least five years' driving experience with two years' experience as a **chauffeur.** You must be at least 25 years old and have a good knowledge of English. Applicants are required to pass a test in English language skills, map reading, and local geography.

### Call 941-555-6367
if interested in applying.

---

**hack license**
(hak LEYE-sehns) a driving permit to drive a taxi or car for hire; also known as a *taxi driver's license*

**chauffeur** (SHOH-fer) a person licensed to drive a car or limousine for hire

---

What is the main idea? The first sentence gives most of the main idea. It is: *The Greenwood Car Service is looking for highly skilled drivers.*

What are the details that support the main idea?

_____

_____

What details can you find in this paragraph? Look at the following phrases: *clean driving record, valid hack license, five years' driving experience, two years' experience as a chauffeur, good knowledge of English, pass a test.*

What do these details have in common? They add information. They all describe requirements. The company wants drivers that meet these requirements. Thus, every detail in the paragraph explains the words *highly skilled drivers.* This is part of the main idea.

Remember, every detail adds in some way to the main idea.

**D**rivers interested in getting their taxi driver's license need to take a test. To find out what is needed to take the test, they may read information like that given below.

## INFORMATION ABOUT
## TAXI DRIVER'S LICENSE EXAMINATION

1. To drive a taxi, or car for hire, state law requires drivers to have a taxi driver's license. To get this license, drivers must pass the Taxi Driver's License Examination. The attached booklet will help you prepare and study for the exam.

2. You must file an exam application in person. Applications can be filed on Monday, Wednesday, and Friday from 9 A.M. to noon and on Tuesday and Thursday from 1 to 5 P.M. The fee is $25, payable in cash or by money order. Bring the following with you when you apply: your driver's license and birth certificate, passport, or other proof that you are legally able to work in the United States.

3. You will receive notification of the date and time of the exam in the mail. To take the exam, bring the following items: your admission card, a pen, your driver's license, and proof that you are legally able to work in the United States (birth certificate, passport, or other papers).

4. The test is made up of five written parts and one oral part. It covers the basic knowledge and skills needed by a taxi driver or chauffeur.

- Part 1 covers motor vehicle laws and safe driving practices.
- Part 2 covers taxicab regulations.
- Part 3 tests your knowledge of local streets and your ability to read street maps.
- Part 4 tests your knowledge of written English. You will have to read street signs, notices, forms, and directions.
- Part 5 is an oral examination. This part tests how well you understand requests spoken in English.

Answer each question based on the reading on page 10. The main idea is given for each paragraph. In the space provided, write two details from the paragraph that support the main idea.

**Example:** Paragraph 1: *The state requires taxi drivers to have a taxi driver's license.*

You must pass the taxi driver's license exam to get a taxi driver's license. The attached booklet will help you prepare and study for the exam.

1. Paragraph 2: *There are specific times, days, and requirements for filing an application for the exam.*

2. Paragraph 3: *You should be prepared for the day of the exam.*

Complete the statement by writing in the correct answer.

3. The main idea of paragraph 4 is

4. How do the bulleted points support the main idea of paragraph 4?

*Check your answers on page 114.*

For years, Alex worked as a taxi driver for a small cab company. He paid a monthly fee to the company to lease, or rent, a taxi. The fee included a charge for upkeep and repairs.

The taxi had a two-way radio so that Alex could get calls from the company dispatcher. The dispatcher sent Alex to different addresses to pick up passengers.

Alex always did well on his taxi shift. He was a good driver who really knew the area. Because English was not his first language, Alex always spoke slowly and clearly. Passengers liked him because he was good-tempered and polite. He earned good tips.

After a while, Alex decided to go into business for himself. The community was growing, and some large new corporations had just opened offices. If he could get some steady work as a driver with the new companies, Alex would do well.

Alex bought a taxi and got a permit to operate it. He was a good mechanic and hoped to do car repairs himself. He also took courses in accounting and business and read books on running a small business.

Alex knew it would take hard work to succeed. He was willing to try because he loved the freedom of being his own boss.

**TALK ABOUT IT**

**1.** Discuss the skills Alex needs to succeed as a taxi driver.

**2.** Describe how Alex's reading skills will help him run his own taxi business.

The Silver Arrow Taxicab Service provides written guidelines for all of its drivers. The guidelines help drivers know what they should do in different situations.

**radio fare** (RAY-dee-oh fair) a passenger assigned by the radio dispatcher

**discriminate** (dih-SKRIHM-ih-nayt) to refuse to serve a customer for reasons such as the customer's race, religion, sex, or ethnic background

**odometer** (oh-DAHM-eht-er) an instrument in a car that records miles

**trip record** (trihp reh-KAWRD) a log showing the details of taxi rides during a shift

**taximeter** (TAK-see-meet-ehr) an instrument in a taxicab that measures distance and computes fares

## GUIDELINES FOR DRIVERS

1. Check in with the office as soon as you arrive. You will be assigned the next available car. Check the car's gas, oil, windshield-washer fluid, and lights. Remember to display your license in the taxi license holder before starting out.
2. If you want to pick up a **radio fare**, call Jeannie to confirm that you are on your way there. Remember that it is illegal to **discriminate** against anyone who wants to hire the taxi.
3. Always greet your passenger and ask for the destination. Write the time, pickup location, and starting **odometer** reading on the **trip record**. Start the **taximeter**.
4. Always take the most direct route. If you think it would be better to take an indirect route, explain why to the passenger. If the passenger prefers another route, follow the request.
5. If your route will take you through a toll booth or beyond city limits, tell the passenger. Ask for the toll money at the start. Explain that the passenger must pay the return trip fare for rides beyond city limits.
6. When you arrive at the destination, turn off the taximeter. Announce the fare. Always give exact change. It's up to the passenger to tip you. Offer a receipt. Then, record the destination and odometer reading on the trip record.
7. If you are ever in an accident, follow these standard procedures. Exchange licenses and registration cards with the other driver. Wait for the arrival of the police. Call the office to report and to get instructions.
8. If the taxicab breaks down, call the office. We may send a mechanic to make repairs on the spot. Or we may send a tow truck to bring you and the taxicab back.

1                                                    GUIDELINES FOR DRIVERS

Answer each question based on the guidelines on page 13. Think about the details in each point of the guidelines. Then, choose the correct main idea.

**1.** Which of the following sums up the main idea of point 1?

    a. You are responsible for your car.
    b. Follow certain steps to get your car ready.
    c. You may not drive without your taxi license.

**2.** Which of the following sums up the main idea of point 2?

    a. There are rules and laws about picking up fares.
    b. Discrimination is illegal.
    c. Let Jeannie know whenever you pick up a fare.

**3.** Which of the following sums up the main idea of point 3?

    a. Customers like to be greeted.
    b. Make sure to do the paperwork.
    c. When picking up a passenger, follow procedure.

**4.** Which of the following sums up the main idea of point 4?

    a. Always take the most direct route.
    b. Take the most direct route unless there are other good reasons not to.
    c. Let the customer pick the most direct route.

**5.** Which of the following sums up the main idea of point 5?

    a. Tell riders about extra costs at the start of the trip.
    b. Passengers should pay all extra costs right away.
    c. Sometimes, there are extra costs for the passengers.

**6.** Which of the following sums up the main idea of point 6?

    a. It is not polite to ask for a tip.
    b. Follow procedures when you arrive at the destination.
    c. Do the paperwork at the end of the trip.

**7.** Which of the following sums up the main idea of point 7?

    a. There are guidelines to follow in case of an accident.
    b. Never leave the scene of an accident.
    c. In an accident, wait for police and follow their instructions.

*Check your answers on page 114.*

# ◆ LESSON WRAP-UP

The details in a paragraph support the main idea. They explain by adding facts and examples. These "specifics" make the main idea clearer.

To check that you understand the main idea of a paragraph, ask yourself questions. Ask how every detail adds to the main idea.

**1.** Imagine that a friend had a job interview. Your friend thinks the interview went well. What details would support your friend's idea that the interview went well? What questions would you ask to find out these details?

**2.** Think of an event that you have attended. It may be a party, a wedding, a concert, or some other event. Imagine that you want to describe the event to a friend.

First, write down the main idea that you want to express. Next, write two details that support the main idea.

Main Idea:

Details:

**3.** Think of a magazine or newspaper article you have read recently. Think of a movie or television show you have seen recently.

First, write down the main idea of the movie, show, or article. Next, write two details that support the main idea.

Main idea:

Details:

*Check your answers on page 114.*

# L e s s o n  3

# Driving Passengers on a Bus

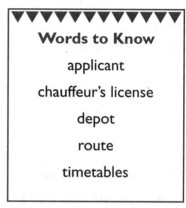

**Words to Know**

applicant

chauffeur's license

depot

route

timetables

Buses provide an important service. Many people don't have a car. Others are too old, young, or sick to drive. Without bus service, these people would find it hard to get to work, school, and other places.

Local transit bus drivers drive daily routes within a community. Their routes may include stops for passengers every few blocks. Intercity bus drivers take people long distances. They travel between cities or regions.

School bus drivers take children to and from school. They work mostly in suburban and rural areas. Nearly three out of four bus drivers work as school bus drivers.

Bus drivers must figure out information from schedules and maps. For example, they might use a schedule to figure out how long a trip should take. This reading skill is called **making inferences**. Workers often need information that is not stated in their reading material. That is why it is important to make inferences.

## Job Focus

**Bus drivers** must be excellent drivers, deal well with people, and use good judgment. Bus drivers follow a schedule and a planned route. However, drivers must be able to make decisions on their own. They need to handle bad weather, traffic jams, and other problems.

Most bus drivers must have a special license. This lets them drive a vehicle that carries passengers. They must pass a special driving test for this license.

About half a million bus drivers are now working. Employment for bus drivers is expected to be good through the year 2005.

# Making Inferences: How It Works

Readers sometimes find ideas that are not stated in what they read. Good readers use clues and hints from their reading to figure out unstated ideas. When readers use clues to add meaning to what they read, they are **making inferences.** Workers often use clues and details in their reading, plus what they already know, to make inferences on the job.

Read the beginning of the employee manual below.

---

## ALL ABOARD!

Welcome to the Golden Arrow team! The Golden Arrow Bus Company was founded in 1975. The founders were Herman and Paul Riccio. They started with just two buses and four bus routes. Today, Golden Arrow is a major bus company. It services eight out of twenty counties in this state.

As a successful **applicant,** you have a **chauffeurs' license** and have passed our difficult written, driving, and physical exams. Now your training period begins. Most companies have a two-week training period. However, Golden Arrow believes in a four-week training program. At the end of the training program, you will take your final exam.

---

**applicant** (AP-lih-kuhnt) a person who asks for a job

**chauffeur's license** (SHOH-ferz LY-sehns) a state-issued license to drive a commercial vehicle such as a bus

The part of the employee manual shown here states that the company was started in 1975. You can get other information that is not stated. How can you infer how long the company has been in business?

*Subtract 1975 from the current year.*

The manual also says that the founders were Herman and Paul Riccio. Herman and Paul Riccio have the same last name. What inference can you make from this? *You can infer that they are from the same family.*

You can also infer ideas and attitudes. The manual describes the company training program. It is longer than that of most companies. The applicant must pass an exam at the end. What can you infer about the Golden Arrow Bus Company's attitude toward training?

*The company takes training very seriously. It seems to expect employees to meet very high standards.*

Besides inferring information from paragraphs, you also can make inferences from visual information such as maps and **timetables.** They sometimes show information more clearly than paragraphs do.

**timetables** (TYM-tay-behl) listings of departure and arrival times for buses, trains, airplanes, or boats; also called schedules

**route** (root) a planned path or course of travel

**depot** (DEE-poh) a place where buses or trains begin their route; also called a terminal or station

Mike works for the Red Comet Bus Company. Next week, he starts driving a new **route.** His supervisor gave him this map and a note.

Mike:

The new route goes from the bus **depot** to City Hall. Unlike your old route, this one goes through downtown, which is a heavy traffic area. Only our best drivers get tough routes like this one. You start this route Monday. Talk to Agnes about a practice run. The round trip is about 17 miles.

Al

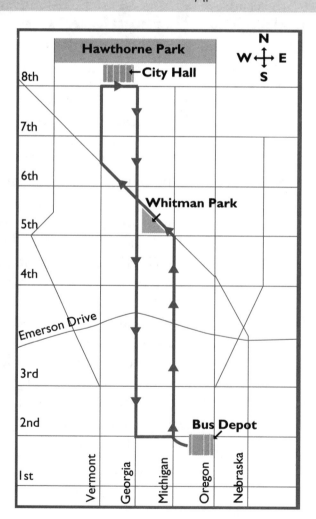

**LESSON 3 ◆ DRIVING PASSENGERS ON A BUS**

Answer each question based on the note and map on page 18.

1. The new route runs

   a. mostly north and south
   b. mostly east and west
   c. on the edge of town

2. Along which street will Mike drive south?

   a. Michigan Avenue
   b. Nebraska Boulevard
   c. Georgia Avenue

3. City Hall is located

   a. at the west end of the route
   b. at the halfway point of the route
   c. next to the depot

4. Name two streets that probably have most of the bus stops along the new route.



5. Which streets border Whitman Park?



Reread the note from Al to Mike. Look for inferences that Mike can make. Then, read the following statements. Circle **Yes** if the note gives enough information to make the inference. Circle **No** if the note does not give enough information to make the inference.

Yes No   **6.** The new route is more difficult than the old route.

Yes No   **7.** Al thinks Mike is one of the company's best drivers.

Yes No   **8.** Al would like to be Mike's friend.

Yes No   **9.** Mike should take a vacation until Monday, when he starts the new route.

Yes No **10.** Agnes can help Mike arrange a practice run.

Yes No **11.** The trip from the depot to City Hall is about $8\frac{1}{2}$ miles.

*Check your answers on page 114.*

Putting on her uniform jacket, Shawna walked out to the waiting bus. She checked the oil and tires on the bus. Then, she boarded the bus and climbed into her seat.

Shawna adjusted the seat and the rearview mirrors and checked the destination sign. Then, she started up the bus in order to check the gas gauge, the windshield wipers, the brakes, and the lights. Finally, Shawna drove up to the bus stop and opened the door to the passengers.

As passengers got on, she took their money, made change, and gave out transfers. She smiled and said hello to her regular passengers. Then, she closed the doors and started off.

Shawna enjoys her job as a local transit bus driver. The work is sometimes stressful. There might be traffic problems or difficult passengers. Still, Shawna likes being in charge of the bus. She likes being outdoors and working with people.

As a city employee, Shawna had to pass a civil service test. She must be able to use maps and schedules. She also reads notices and instructions about new procedures.

Like the other bus drivers, Shawna joined the municipal bus drivers' union. She pays union dues and receives union benefits. For example, the union often bargains with the city for pay raises. Shawna feels that she has a good job at a good salary.

## TALK ABOUT IT

1. Explain what is stressful about Shawna's job.

2. Tell why Shawna likes her job.

3. Describe the kinds of materials Shawna must read.

Drivers who drive the Route 17 bus line use the following information to stay on schedule along the route.

## ROUTE 17—WEEKDAY MORNING TIMETABLE

| Bus No. | Depot | Stop 1 | Stop 2 | Stop 3 | Stop 4 | Stop 5 | Stop 6 |
|---------|-------|--------|--------|--------|--------|--------|--------|
| 1701 | 6:00 | 6:10 | 6:23 | 6:35 | 6:46 | 6:59 | 7:11 |
| 1702 | 6:30 | 6:40 | 6:53 | 7:05 | 7:16 | 7:29 | 7:41 |
| 1703 | 7:00 | 7:10 | 7:23 | 7:35 | 7:46 | 7:59 | 8:11 |
| 1704 | 7:30 | 7:40 | 7:53 | 8:05 | 8:16 | 8:29 | 8:41 |
| 1705 | 8:00 | 8:11 | 8:25 | 8:38 | 8:50 | 9:04 | 9:17 |
| 1706 | 8:20 | 8:31 | 8:45 | 8:58 | 9:10 | 9:24 | 9:37 |
| 1707 | 8:40 | 8:51 | 9:05 | 9:18 | 9:30 | 9:44 | 9:57 |
| 1708 | 9:00 | 9:11 | 9:25 | 9:38 | 9:50 | 10:04 | 10:17 |
| 1709 | 9:20 | 9:32 | 9:47 | 10:01 | 10:14 | 10:29 | 10:43 |
| 1710 | 9:40 | 9:52 | 10:07 | 10:21 | 10:34 | 10:49 | 11:03 |
| 1711 | 10:00 | 10:12 | 10:27 | 10:41 | 10:54 | 11:09 | 11:23 |
| 1712 | 11:00 | 11:12 | 11:27 | 11:41 | 11:54 | **12:09** | **12:23** |

Note: Boldface type means P.M. (afternoon). All buses leave from the Allen Street depot.

STOP 1  Allen and Williams Streets
STOP 2  Allen and Emerson Streets
STOP 3  Emerson St. and M. L. King Jr. Boulevard

STOP 4  M. L. King Jr. Boulevard and Seminole Avenue
STOP 5  M. L. King Jr. Boulevard and Jefferson Street
STOP 6  Jefferson Street and Roosevelt Circle

## CHECK YOUR UNDERSTANDING

Answer each question based on the schedule above.

**1.** How many buses cover Route 17 on weekday mornings?

    a. 12
    b. 8
    c. 6

**2.** How many stops does a bus make after leaving the depot?

    a. 12
    b. 7
    c. 6

**3.** What does the bus number tell you?

    a. the number of buses on the route
    b. the time the bus left the depot
    c. the bus route and times

**4.** Along which street are there the most stops?

a. Emerson Street
b. Williams Street
c. M. L. King Jr. Boulevard

**5.** How many buses on this schedule make stops after noon?

a. all
b. two
c. one

For each statement, figure out which bus the passenger should take and what time the passenger should get the bus.

**Example:** A passenger wants to get a bus at Stop 4 and arrive at Stop 6 by 9:40.

Bus no.: <u>1706</u>          Time: <u>9:10</u>

**6.** A passenger wants to get a bus at Stop 3 and arrive at Stop 5 before 7:30.

Bus no.: _____          Time: _____

**7.** A passenger wants to get a bus at Stop 1 and arrive at Stop 4 by 10:30.

Bus no.: _____          Time: _____

**8.** A passenger wants to get a bus at Stop 2 and arrive at Stop 5 no later than 9:00.

Bus no.: _____          Time: _____

**9.** A passenger arrived 5 minutes early for a 9:30 meeting near the corner of Allen and Emerson Streets. Which bus did the passenger probably take? Bus no.: _____

**10.** A passenger was to meet a friend near Jefferson Street and Roosevelt Circle at 11:00. The passenger arrived about 20 minutes late. Which bus did the passenger probably take? Bus no.: _____

*Check your answers on page 115.*

# ◆ LESSON WRAP-UP

Making inferences is a way of finding out ideas that are not stated directly. You can uncover information by looking for clues and hints. You can infer ideas and attitudes from your reading. You can infer information from words and from numbers.

**I.** We make inferences from what we read and already know. Imagine that you find yourself in each of the following situations.

In each case, make an inference from the information given.

    a. All children must be vaccinated before starting
       school. Your niece plans to start school next year.
You would infer that



    b. Your friend Elena has invited you over for dinner.
       Elena does not eat meat or fish.
You would infer that



**2.** Making inferences is sometimes called "reading between the lines." This means that you are getting information that is not stated directly.

Imagine that you have received the following message from a friend. Write an idea that you get by reading between the lines.

> Hi!
>     I found a new apartment that is exactly what I wanted. I have to move out of my old place by October 31. The problem is this: I don't have enough money to pay for movers. Johnny is willing to lend me his van, but I need to find at least four strong friends to help me move. Do you know of anyone who could help?
>                    Jean

By reading between the lines, I see that

*Check your answers on page 115.*

# L e s s o n   4

# Selling Tickets

Have you ever been to a baseball game, concert, or amusement park? Before you can enter any of these places, you must buy a ticket.

Ticket sellers work in a wide variety of places. When they sell tickets face to face, they are often in a booth or small office. Zoos, amusement parks, movie theaters, fairs, and museums are some of the businesses that sell most of their tickets at the door.

However, tickets to concerts, stage plays, and major league ballgames may be sold over the telephone.

When customers ask questions, ticket sellers need to give quick, correct information. They must be able to find information on charts, seating plans, and other items. **Understanding visual information** is a valuable reading skill that ticket sellers must have. They need this skill in order to give customers important details about the tickets they buy.

## Job Focus

**Ticket sellers** work with the public all day. They need to be courteous and helpful. Some customers may be undecided or impatient when buying tickets. It is important to try to serve each customer as quickly and politely as possible.

To sell tickets, ticket sellers must be able to find information quickly. They have to read schedules, price lists, seating plans, and other materials. They should be able to understand this information and explain it clearly.

Ticket sellers who gain experience and skill may decide to move into sales or supervisory jobs.

# Understanding Visual Information: How It Works

Diagrams and charts are two forms of visual information. A chart contains columns of information in words or numbers. Examples of items in a chart are dates, days of the week, and times. To understand information in a chart, use the words at the tops of the columns. These words are the column headings. They help you find the information you need.

A diagram shows information using both words and pictures. Words and numbers may be used to label, or identify, parts of a diagram. To understand a diagram, find the labels that tell you what you want to know.

The chart below lists home games in June for a local baseball team. Read the information in the chart.

| Ridgewood Stars Home Games | | | |
|---|---|---|---|
| Date | Day | Opponent | Time |
| June 21 | Mon. | Middletown Bears | 7:00 p.m. |
| June 22 | Tues. | Middletown Bears | 7:00 p.m. |
| June 25 | Fri. | Hudson Redwings | 7:00 p.m. |
| June 26 | Sat. | Hudson Redwings | 7:00 p.m. |
| June 27 | Sun. | Oceana Dolphins | 1:30 p.m. |
| June 28 | Mon. | Oceana Dolphins | 7:00 p.m. |

A customer asks, "How many Sunday games are there in June?" How can you use the chart to answer the question?

Look under the column heading "Day." The days of the games are listed there. Then, add up the number of games listed for Sundays.

_____

*The total is one.* You have found details in the chart to answer the question.

Another customer asks, "Are there any afternoon games in June?" You know that *afternoon* means between noon and evening. You can look at the information under the heading "Time." Can you find an afternoon game?

_____

*There is one game that will start at 1:30 P.M.* Your answer to the customer can be "There is one afternoon game at 1:30 P.M. on Sunday, June 27."

any important details can be found using a visual diagram like the following seating map.

**Marlowe Theater Seating**

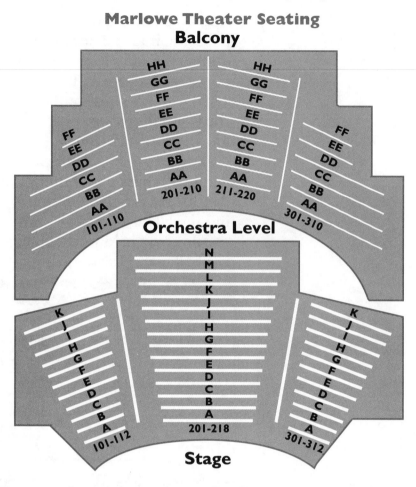

**balcony** (BAL-kuh-nee) an upper level of a theater that extends from the back wall part way over the lower level

**orchestra level** (AWR-kihs-truh lehv-ehl) the main floor of a theater

Every seat has a letter and a number. For example, seat DD-203 is in row DD in the **balcony** section for seats 201-210. Seat A-201 is in row A on the **orchestra level** for seats 201-218.

## CHECK YOUR UNDERSTANDING

Answer each question based on the diagram above.

1. How many rows of seats are there in the center of the orchestra (seats 201-218)?

    a. 11          b. 14          c. 36

2. How many rows of seats are there for seats 301-310 in the balcony?

    a. 6          b. 10          c. 26

3. How many BB seats are there altogether in the theater?

    a. 10          b. 20          c. 40

**LESSON 4 ◆ SELLING TICKETS**

**4.** A customer would like orchestra level seats. Which of the following available seats would you offer: K-202 to K-210, FF-219 to FF-220, or DD-109 to DD-110?

**5.** A customer asks, "Does seat K-105 face the right or the left of the stage?"

**6.** A customer asks, "Which seat is closer to the stage: M-206 or F-301?"

**7.** A customer needs six seats together. Would you offer BB-204 to BB-210 or BB-211 to BB-216?

*Check your answers on page 115.*

## ON THE JOB

Early morning was the best time at the zoo for Alberto. The air was cool and filled with animal noises. He set up the ticket booth for a busy day.

Alberto read and put out notices about upcoming events. He wrote the day's special activities on a large board. He checked the list of fees for the day.

When the zoo opened, people lined up at the ticket booth. Alberto handed out tickets, took money, and made change. He gave every visitor a map of the zoo. Pleasantly and calmly, Alberto answered many questions about special exhibits, animal feeding times, and the zoo gift shop.

### TALK ABOUT IT

**1.** Discuss how reading helps Alberto prepare for the day.

**2.** Describe how Alberto helps visitors to the zoo.

any places list their entrance fees using a price chart like this.

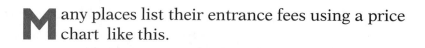

## CRYSTAL LAKE
### AMUSEMENT PARK

May 30 to September 30

| | Weekends and Holidays | Weekdays |
|---|---|---|
| Adults | $10.00 | $7.50 |
| Senior citizens* | 8.00 | 6.00 |
| Children 2-12 years | 5.00 | 3.75 |
| Children under 2 | 2.00 | 1.00 |

*Seniors citizens must be 65 or older to qualify for lower fees.
School groups of 15 or more: 10 percent **discount.**
Baby strollers available **gratis.**

**discount** (DIHS-kownt)
a reduction in price

**gratis** (GRAYT-ihs) free of charge

## CHECK YOUR UNDERSTANDING

Circle **True** or **False** for each statement based on the price chart.

True  False  1. Tickets are cheaper on Wednesday than on Sunday.

True  False  2. Tickets for kids under 2 are half price on weekdays.

True  False  3. A senior citizen would pay $6.00 on July 4.

True  False  4. There is a 10 percent discount for any group of 15 or more.

True  False  5. Baby strollers are available for a small charge.

True  False  6. Admission prices are the same all year-round.

Use the price chart to figure out fees for the following groups visiting the Crystal Lake Amusement Park.

**Example:** a group of two adults and two children on a holiday
2 x $10 = $20; 2 x $5 = $10; $20 + $10 = $30 total

7. three 18-year-olds on a Saturday evening

**8.** a mother, her 9-year-old, and 2-year-old on a Tuesday afternoon

**9.** 6-year-old twins with their 60-year-old grandmother on a Sunday afternoon

*Check your answers on page 115.*

## ◆ LESSON WRAP-UP

Charts and diagrams are ways of showing information in a visual form. It is important to be able to use these different forms of information to find important details. For example, a big part of a ticket seller's job is to answer customers' questions and help them compare details. A customer may want to compare prices and locations of different seats for a concert. Being able to locate important details quickly and correctly will help make the customer happy.

**1.** You see charts and diagrams in everyday life. You might see them in a restaurant or at a movie theater. Think about what kind of information you see on such charts.

Write a few sentences about using a price chart at a movie theater to find important details.

**2.** Think about different schedules that you might find helpful. They can be class schedules, ballgame schedules, or even TV program schedules. Choose a kind of schedule that you would use.

Write a few sentences about the important details you would find using the schedule.

*Check your answers on page 115.*

# ◆ UNIT ONE REVIEW

**1.** Write a brief paragraph that explains how to find the main idea of a paragraph. Be sure to describe the difference between a topic and a main idea.

**2.** Imagine that you are writing a paragraph with this main idea: "Finding a job is hard work." Write three details you would use to support this main idea.

a.

b.

c.

**3.** Write a definition of *making inferences*. Give an example that supports your definition.

**4.** List three different visuals that can be used to organize information. Give an example of the kind of information you might organize in each of the visuals you list.

a.

b.

c.

*Check your answers on page 115.*

# Jobs Working with Children

Jobs for people who work with children include child-care providers, classroom assistants, counselors, and coaches. Child-care workers take care of young children when the parents cannot. Classroom assistants help the teacher and students. Coaches and counselors take care of children in camps and after-school programs.

People who work with children, like all employees, need good reading skills. In this unit, a child-care provider must follow the directions given by a city agency. A classroom assistant follows a classroom schedule written by the teacher. A coach must tell the difference between facts and opinions in a coach's handbook.

This unit teaches the following reading skills:

- following directions in lists and paragraphs
- following directions on schedules and agendas
- distinguishing fact from opinion

You will learn how people who work with children use these reading skills in their work.

# Providing Child-Care Services

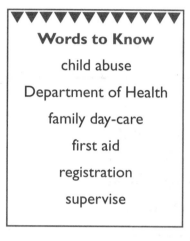

**▼▼▼▼▼▼▼▼▼▼▼▼**
**Words to Know**

child abuse

Department of Health

family day-care

first aid

registration

supervise

When parents work, they cannot take care of their children full time. Some parents rely on relatives or friends. Many others rely on child-care providers. A child-care provider takes care of young children when parents cannot.

Child-care providers are valuable workers. Without them, many parents would not be able to go to work. Parents value a child-care provider's good judgment.

Like other workers, a child-care provider must be able to **follow directions** on the job. Directions tell how to do something. They can appear in a list, on a schedule, or in another form. For example, a child-care provider might take a child for a medical checkup. The parent may have left written directions to the doctor's office. The child-care provider must read and follow the directions.

## Job Focus

Many **child-care providers** work in a day-care center. The center is a homelike place where children eat, play, and nap. There is usually one worker for every four or five children.

The providers play with the children and read to them. They feed the children and keep them clean. Most important, they comfort and guide the children.

To be a child-care provider, you need patience and energy. You should enjoy playing with children and helping them learn. You must be dependable and show good judgment.

There are more than one million preschool teachers and day-care workers in the United States. The number of jobs is expected to increase through the year 2005.

# Following Directions: How It Works

Writing that tells how to do a task is called *instructions* or *directions*. **Following directions** is the skill of understanding instructions and doing what they say.

Directions are usually given in steps. Sometimes, the steps are numbered. Numbers tell you in what order to do the steps. A picture, or diagram, may appear with the directions. These drawings can help you follow certain steps.

When you read directions, follow these steps:

- **Preview the directions:** Read through all the directions first. Make sure to look at any diagrams.
- **Prepare for the tasks:** Gather the needed materials.
- **Follow the directions:** Do the tasks in order.
- **Review your work:** Ask yourself, "Did I get the right results?" If there are problems, read the directions again. Look at the directions for mixing baby formula.

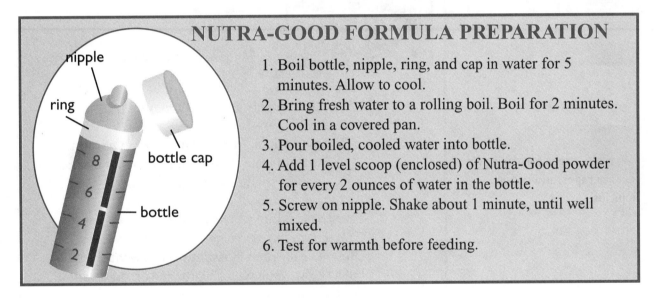

## NUTRA-GOOD FORMULA PREPARATION

1. Boil bottle, nipple, ring, and cap in water for 5 minutes. Allow to cool.
2. Bring fresh water to a rolling boil. Boil for 2 minutes. Cool in a covered pan.
3. Pour boiled, cooled water into bottle.
4. Add 1 level scoop (enclosed) of Nutra-Good powder for every 2 ounces of water in the bottle.
5. Screw on nipple. Shake about 1 minute, until well mixed.
6. Test for warmth before feeding.

What materials are needed?

_____

_____

*A scoop, formula, bottle, nipple, ring, cap, covered pan, and water are needed.*

How much time do you think it would take to prepare a bottle of formula?

_____

Boil the equipment (5 minutes), boil fresh water (2 minutes), and shake the bottle (1 minute). *It will take at least 8 minutes to prepare the formula.*

Why do you think a drawing comes with the directions?

---

*The drawing helps you to understand the first step. It is also a quick reminder.*

**supervise** (SOO-pehr-veyez) to watch over or control

Alex works at the South Side Day-Care Center. He and two other workers will take 15 children to the Dinosaur Playground. Alex will help **supervise** the children. The playground has a sandbox, climbing equipment, and swings. The group plans to walk to the playground after the children awake from their nap at about 1:30 P.M. The director has written a list of instructions for the trip.

**first aid** steps for caring for cuts, scrapes, and other injuries

South Side Day-Care Center

Dinosaur Playground Trip

Pack the following items:
1. snacks (apple juice and crackers)
2. sand toys
3. extra pants (in case the children get wet)
4. **first aid** box (supplies for cuts and scrapes)
5. tissues, towels, and cups

Wake the children.
Take the children to the bathroom.
Give Jimmy his medicine.
Dress the children in sweaters or sweatshirts.
Put the five youngest children in the kiddie cart.
Lock up and leave.

## CHECK YOUR UNDERSTANDING

Answer each question based on the list of instructions above.

1. What is the first instruction?

   a. Take the children to the bathroom.
   b. Pack the following items.
   c. Wake the children.

**2.** What must the child-care providers do just after waking the children?

    a. Pack the supplies.

    b. Dress the children in warm clothes.

    c. Take the children to the bathroom.

**3.** Which of the following will not be packed for the trip?

    a. baseballs and bats

    b. snacks

    c. first aid box

**4.** What is the last instruction to be followed before the group locks up and leaves?

    a. Take the children to the bathroom.

    b. Put the five youngest children in the kiddie cart.

    c. Give Jimmy his medicine.

**5.** What will the children have for a snack?

    a. ice cream

    b. something bought on the way to the playground

    c. apple juice and crackers

**6.** How would you probably learn how much medicine to give to Jimmy?

    a. Ask Jimmy.

    b. Read the medicine label.

    c. Make a guess.

**7.** Which sentence best describes the list of instructions?

    a. You can do the instructions in any order.

    b. You should do the instructions in the order in which they are listed.

    c. You cannot understand the instructions without a diagram.

**8.** How would numbering the list of instructions make it easier to use?

**9.** If the list of instructions were numbered, would you also number the items to be packed? Explain why or why not.

*Check your answers on page 116.*

It was 7:30 A.M. on a bright spring morning. Nicki knocked at the door of the Happy World Child-Care Center. She was thinking about taking the children to the park. The weather would be great for playing outdoors. It was the first real day of spring weather.

Nicki loves working with children. She really enjoys her job as a child-care provider. At the center, Nicki greets children in the morning, gives them snacks and meals, and helps them dress for outdoor play.

The director plans the day's activities. Then, Nicki helps with games, art work, building blocks, and other projects. She also comforts children who are hurt or upset and gently corrects children who misbehave.

To get her job in a day-care center, Nicki took courses in child development and first aid. *Child development* describes how a child changes mentally, physically, and emotionally as he or she grows older. Nicki learned a lot of useful information. For example, she learned how to help a child who cries when the parent leaves.

On the job, Nicki must read and use math skills. She must read daily schedules, special instructions, notes from parents, first aid instructions, and medicine labels. She must sometimes read instructions on child-care equipment. Finally, Nicki often reads storybooks to the children. Nicki enjoys that reading best of all.

## TALK ABOUT IT

**1.** Describe three kinds of instructions Nicki reads on the job.

**2.** Do you think Nicki has an important job? Discuss why or why not.

**A**nita wants to start her own child-care business. She plans to care for a few children in her own home. Anita called the **Department of Health** for information. The Department of Health sent her a brochure. Read the information below.

**Department of Health**
a city or state government office that protects people's health

**family day-care** a small business in which a person provides care for children in his or her home

**registration**
(rej-ih-STRAY-shun) an official listing or record

**child abuse** (uh-BYOOS) cruel or physically harmful acts against children; child abuse is a crime

## What Is Family Day-Care?

Family Day-Care is . . .

- caring for three to six children
- in your own home
- for more than three hours a day

You may care for . . .
- no more than six children over age two **or**
- no more than four children over age two and one child under age two **or**
- no more than three children over age two and two children under age two

The total number of children . . .
- includes your own children under age six
- may not include more than two children under age two

## How Do I Register My Family Day-Care Business?

Please register your **family day-care** business with the Department of Health. **Registration** shows parents that your home is safe for their children. You also can get free training and support if you register.

1. Call 555-3768 Wednesday through Friday between 10 A.M. and 2 P.M. to make a registration appointment.

2. Complete and submit the Registration Application that you receive at the appointment.

3. Submit a State Central Register form for a **child abuse** background check.

4. Submit a Medical Record form for yourself and other household members.

5. Submit a Request for Fire Department Approval form.

6. Attend an information and training workshop.

Answer each question based on the handbook on page 37.

1. Which of the following is a family day-care business?
   a. A teenager baby-sits for a neighbor's child every Saturday night in the neighbor's house.
   b. A man takes his nephew to the playground two afternoons a week while the mother goes to school.
   c. A woman cares for her own baby and two other children in her home every day from 8:00 A.M. to 2:00 P.M.

2. Which statement is *not* true? The total number of children in family day-care
   a. includes the provider's own children under age six.
   b. may include no more than two children under age two.
   c. must be at least age six.

3. Circle the only time that Anita can call to make a registration appointment.
   a. Wednesday at 3:00 P.M.
   b. Wednesday at 11:00 A.M.
   c. Friday at 10:15 P.M.

4. What is the first step Anita must take to register her family day-care business?

5. How many different types of forms must Anita submit during registration? What are they called?

6. What must Anita do *after* she submits a Request for Fire Department Approval form?

7. What is one benefit of registration for the provider? What is one benefit of registration for the parent?

*Check your answers on page 116.*

# ◆ LESSON WRAP-UP

Following directions is an important skill in every job. Sometimes, the instructions are printed, as in a handbook. Sometimes, they are written by hand or typed for a special purpose. In every case, workers must read and understand the instructions before doing the task.

To follow directions, read through the instructions first. Look for help in the pictures that come with the instructions. Make sure you have everything you need. Understand each step before you do it.

**1.** In everyday life, there are many times when we must follow written directions. Think of an experience that you have had following written directions. Perhaps you put together a toy. Perhaps you followed directions on a box of cake mix. Was it easy to follow the directions? Were there pictures or diagrams? Were the instructions numbered? What steps can you take to make it easier to follow directions?

**Finish the sentence below.**

It is easier to follow directions when I

**2.** Workers in all jobs must be able to follow directions. However, sometimes we have trouble getting the directions right. How can we help ourselves follow directions? How can we get help from others?

**Write a paragraph explaining what you can do when you are having trouble following directions.**

*Check your answers on page 116.*

# Lesson 6

# Helping in the Classroom

▼▼▼▼▼▼▼▼▼▼▼
**Words to Know**

auditorium

conference

paraprofessional

superintendent

teacher's aide

An elementary school is a busy place. Young children are learning many skills that will help them succeed in school. They learn how to work in groups and follow directions. They make new friends.

Sometimes, a teacher needs help from a classroom assistant. The teacher may write directions about the day's activities. A good assistant can follow the teacher's directions. Each day's activities may be different. To help the teacher, a classroom assistant must have good reading skills.

Do you write directions to yourself on a calendar? Maybe you list doctors' appointments, birthdays, and other important events. Calendar notes remind you of things you plan to do.

In the classroom, an assistant must read the teacher's calendar notes and **follow the directions.** Then, the assistant must decide how and when to prepare for the day's activities.

## Job Focus

If you enjoy helping others learn, working as a **classroom assistant** can be very rewarding. The day is filled with many activities. You can feel good when the children learn and do well.

However, classroom work takes energy and patience. You must be prepared for messes and noise. You have to control the children. And you must respond to the teacher's needs.

The number of children in school is expected to increase through the year 2000. However, schools will continue to need classroom assistants. Also, classroom experience can lead to other jobs working with children or in education.

# Following Directions: How It Works

One written form of directions is the agenda. An agenda, or schedule, is "a list of activities with the times that the activities will take place." For example, an agenda item for a meeting might be as follows: "10:15–Coffee Break." Sometimes, an agenda also tells you where the events will take place and who will join in the events.

Think of a schedule as directions that plan out your time. Below is a schedule for parent-teacher conferences. How could a teacher use the schedule to prepare for the meetings?

**conference** (KAHN-fer-ehns) a meeting between two or more people to talk about a specific subject

| PARENT-TEACHER **CONFERENCES** | |
|---|---|
| 1:30 | Mr. and Mrs. Sanjay |
| 1:45 | Natasha and Paul Taveras |
| 2:00 | Evelyn Chu |
| 2:15 | Maureen O'Donnell |
| 2:30 | Ms. Palmeros |

**Step 1: Preview the schedule.** Read through the schedule as soon as you get it. Reading the schedule gives a lot of information right away. Can you tell from the schedule how long each conference should be?

---

Yes. You can tell by looking at the times scheduled. *Each conference will take 15 minutes.*

**Step 2: Prepare your work.** After reading the schedule, you can prepare for the activities. For example, the conference schedule shows which parents are coming to talk about their children. To prepare, you would have to think about each student and his or her work. You also would write down comments to tell the parents.

**Step 3: Review the schedule.** Throughout the day, you would keep reviewing the schedule and checking the time.

What can you do if the conference with Evelyn Chu goes on for too long?

---

You might say, *"Let's arrange another meeting on another day to finish this discussion."* In that way, the schedule is kept and the other parents are not left waiting.

Every morning Amelia, the classroom assistant, goes over the classroom schedule for the day. The schedule gives directions how the children will spend their time. Look at the schedule that the class will follow on Wednesday.

| | Wednesday, November 24 |
|---|---|
| 9:00 | Meeting time |
| 9:20 | Science project—planting seeds |
| 10:00 | Group A—Library visit |
| | Group B—Number skills |
| 10:20 | Snack time |
| 10:40 | Playground |
| 11:00 | Music room with music teacher |
| 11:30 | Free play |
| 12:00 | Lunch |
| 12:45 | Rest time |
| 1:15 | Playground |
| 2:00 | Story time |
| 2:30 | Dismissal |

## CHECK YOUR UNDERSTANDING

Answer each question based on the schedule above. Underline **True** if a statement is true or **False** if it is false.

True   False   **1.** Meeting time is the first activity.

True   False   **2.** Lunch is at 1:00.

True   False   **3.** At 10:00, all the children have the same activity.

True   False   **4.** Rest time is right after lunch.

Write your answer to each question in the space provided.

**5.** It takes 10 minutes to get the children ready to go outside. When should Amelia start helping the children get ready for dismissal?

**6.** It is Amelia's job to take the children to different activities in the school. What information does Amelia need to perform her job for group A at 10:00?

_____

_____

**7.** Between 10:20 and 10:40, Amelia will do the following tasks for snack time. In what order should she perform the tasks? Use the letters A through D to show the order. The first one has been done as an example.

____ Dress the children to go outside.

____ Give the children juice and crackers.

_A_ Set the tables for snack.

____ Clean off the tables and put away the food.

*Check your answers on page 116.*

## ON THE JOB

Edna watched the classroom activity. The children were hard at work. The whole kindergarten class was making paper turkeys for Thanksgiving. Edna helped with glue, paper, and crayons.

It is Edna's job to get the materials ready for projects and to clean up afterwards. Edna's job also involves reading the teacher's schedules and directions. She reads notes from parents and from the school staff. She also reads the labels on different things used in class. Because of Edna's work, the teacher has more time to teach.

Edna helps with other tasks. She helps children put on boots in the winter and watches them in the playground. When children are hurt, she comforts them. When children misbehave, she corrects them.

The teacher depends on Edna's help, and Edna enjoys working closely with the teacher to make the class a success. When she sees how much the children learn and grow, Edna feels very good about her job.

### TALK ABOUT IT

**1.** Describe how important reading is on Edna's job.

**2.** Name three kinds of materials Edna needs to read.

**paraprofessional**
(pair-uh-proh-FEHSH-un-al) a specially trained person who works with teachers, lawyers, or other professionals

The Board of Education announced a half-day training conference for **paraprofessionals.** This was a chance for Mark, a classroom assistant, to learn new skills and talk to others about the job.

When he arrived, Mark received an agenda for the conference. He noticed that he had a choice of sessions to attend at 9:40 and at 10:40. Look at the agenda, and answer the questions that follow.

---

**BOARD OF EDUCATION**

## PARAPROFESSIONALS' TRAINING CONFERENCE

Education Board Building ◻ January 20

*Agenda*

| | |
|---|---|
| 8:30-9:00 | Registration—Coffee and Pastry Buffet; Conference Room |
| 9:00-9:40 | **Teacher's Aides**—Opportunity and Responsibility; **Auditorium** Speaker: **Superintendent** Ruben Suarez |
| 9:40-10:20 | Session A—Working with Difficult Children; Room 120 Session B—Safety in the Playground; Room 124 |
| 10:20-10:40 | Coffee Break; Conference Room |
| 10:40-11:20 | Session A—Creative Children; Room 124 Session B—How Children Make Friends; Room 120 |
| 11:20-12:00 | Education for the Future; Auditorium Speaker: Assistant Superintendent Margaret Chin |
| 12:00-1:00 | Box Lunch; Conference Room |

---

**teacher's aide** a person who works in a classroom helping the teacher

**auditorium** (aw-dih-TAWR-ee-um) a large room with many seats

**superintendent** (soo-per-ihn-TEN-duhnt) a supervisor of a school system

---

## CHECK YOUR UNDERSTANDING

Answer each question based on the agenda above.

1. Which two sessions are given at 9:40?

2. How long is the 11:20 speech?

**3.** How many hours will the entire conference take?

**4.** Who is the speaker scheduled for 9:00?

**5.** A child in Mark's class takes medication that makes him restless. Which session might help Mark with this problem?

**6.** The teacher in Mark's class is always looking for new projects. Which session might help Mark with project ideas?

*Check your answers on page 116.*

## ◆ LESSON WRAP-UP

Schedules help you prepare for the day's tasks. They also help you keep track of your work. On most jobs, parts of the schedule stay the same each day. However, some activities change from day to day. Workers must be prepared for the changes.

To use a schedule, remember to:
- Preview: Read the schedule.
- Prepare: Write down what you must do.
- Review: Check the schedule often.

**1.** Write a schedule for yourself to follow on the day of a job interview. Include planning how to get there, getting ready, and giving yourself enough time to get to the interview early.

**2.** Look at the agenda you wrote for yourself. Choose one activity that you could break down into smaller steps. Write a brief paragraph explaining how you would give yourself more specific reminders about getting ready.

*Check your answers on page 117.*

# Coaching and Counseling Children

▼▼▼▼▼▼▼▼▼▼▼▼
**Words to Know**

campers

counselor

day camp

evaluation report

Many children attend programs after school and during the summer. These programs range from after-school clubs to summer camps. In these youth programs, children do many different activities. There may be arts and crafts, drama, and music projects. Sports activities are a major part of most programs.

A camp counselor (KOWN-sehl-ehr) is usually in charge of a group of children for most of the day. The counselor makes sure that the children get from one activity to another. Counselors also may supervise activities. A coach is usually in charge of any sports activities.

For both counselors and coaches, **distinguishing fact from opinion** is an important skill. For example, if two children have an argument, the coach or counselor must distinguish what really happened (fact) from what each child thinks happened (opinion).

Telling facts from opinions is also an important reading skill. In this lesson you will read some job materials to help you decide what makes facts differ from opinions.

## Job Focus

Working in a youth program requires patience, dedication, and a love of children. You want the children to have a good time and to learn skills. You also would be responsible for the safety and well-being of the group.

To work in a youth program, you may need training in coaching children.

**Coaches** work at community centers. They also work in summer camps and after-school programs. As more parents hold full-time jobs, the need for these programs will increase.

# Distinguishing Fact from Opinion: How It Works

Writing contains information. Some of the information is fact while other information is opinion. **Distinguishing fact from opinion** means telling the difference between facts (which can be proven) and opinions (which cannot be proven).

Facts can be proven by experience or observation. Read the following statement: "There are 20 people in the room." If the number of people is proven to be true by counting, the statement is a fact.

A statement of fact involves things that exist or happen, such as names, numbers, places, and events.

- The chair is made of oak.
- They decided to buy the car.
- His parents were married on June 20, 1960.

An opinion is a belief or judgment. Different people can have different opinions about the same fact. The following statements are opinions:

- "The car they bought is the best." The words *the best* show the writer's judgment. What may seem like the best to one person may seem like the worst to another.
- "The car they bought won't last long." Beliefs about the future are opinions, not facts.

The Notice to Counselors below contains both facts and opinions. Read the notice.

**counselor** (KOWN-suh-luhr) a person who supervises people at a camp

**campers** (KAMP-erz) people going to camp

---

NOTICE TO **COUNSELORS**
As you know, a trip to Nelson's Orchard to pick cherries has been planned for Friday. Since the weather report predicts rain, **campers** should wear rain gear. You should pack extra ponchos in your bags.

---

**What are the facts?**
- *A trip has been planned.* (decision)
- *The trip is to Nelson's Orchard.* (place)
- *The day of the trip is Friday.* (date)

**What are the opinions?**
- *Rain gear should be worn.* (judgment)
- *You should pack ponchos.* (judgment)

**day camp** a place where children go for sports and play during the day in the summer

**evaluation report** (ee-val-yoo-AY-shun) a written form that gives facts and opinions about a person or situation

Robert works at Hawk's Crest **Day Camp.** The day camp provides summer activities for children who are on vacation from school. The children play sports and do other activities during the day. They go home at night.

Robert coaches the sports teams. He meets many children. He also works with the children's counselors. Each counselor is in charge of one group of children for the whole day.

Counselors fill out an **evaluation report** for each camper. The report tells how well the child is doing at camp. Robert must add his evaluation to each report.

The camp director gave Robert a sample evaluation report. Read the following report.

---

# Hawk's Crest Day Camp
## E v a l u a t i o n   R e p o r t

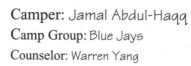

**Camper:** Jamal Abdul-Haqq    **Date:** July 7
**Camp Group:** Blue Jays    **Age:** 9
**Counselor:** Warren Yang    **Coach:** Rosalind Hernandez

### SWIMMING
Level 3—Jamal can swim the width of the pool and back without stopping. He can tread water for one minute. He needs to work on his breathing skills.

### SPORTS
Jamal is great at softball. He has the most hits on his team. He needs to work on his fielding skills. Jamal works very hard at tennis. He has come to all the extra practices. He needs to work on his form.

### ARTS AND CRAFTS
Jamal has finished three projects. His work is colorful and original. He made a great puppet for the puppet show.

### MUSIC AND DRAMA
Jamal is learning the recorder. He can play "Old MacDonald." He told me playing music was fun. He's a fast learner.

### SOCIAL SKILLS
Jamal plays well with other children. He doesn't fight or tease. He seems popular with other children.

There is one small problem. Sometimes he doesn't want to follow instructions. I must ask him two or three times.

### COMMENTS
Jamal is a wonderful boy. He knows what he likes and works hard. It's a pleasure to have him in the group.

---

Answer each question based on the report on page 48. Underline **Fact** if the statement is a fact or **Opinion** if it is an opinion.

**Example** Swimming:

<u>Fact</u> **Opinion**   Jamal can tread water for one minute.

**Fact** <u>Opinion</u>   Jamal needs to work on his breathing skills.

1. Sports:

**Fact Opinion**   a. Jamal has the most hits on his team.
**Fact Opinion**   b. Jamal needs to work on fielding skills.
**Fact Opinion**   c. Jamal works very hard at tennis.

2. Arts and Crafts:

**Fact Opinion**   a. Jamal has finished three projects.
**Fact Opinion**   b. Jamal's work is colorful and original.
**Fact Opinion**   c. Jamal's puppet was great.

3. Music and Drama:

**Fact Opinion**   a. Jamal is learning to play the recorder.
**Fact Opinion**   b. Jamal can play "Old MacDonald."
**Fact Opinion**   c. Jamal is a fast learner.

4. Social Skills:

**Fact Opinion**   a. Jamal plays well with other children.
**Fact Opinion**   b. Jamal doesn't fight or tease.
**Fact Opinion**   c. Jamal seems popular with other children.

Each statement in quotation marks (" ") contains a fact and an opinion. Circle the letter of the fact in the statement.

5. "Jamal told me playing music was fun."

   a. Jamal said something positive to the counselor.
   b. Music lessons are fun.
   c. Jamal is learning a lot from the music lessons.

6. "Jamal made a great puppet for the puppet show."

   a. Jamal's puppet was beautiful.
   b. Jamal made a puppet for the puppet show.
   c. Everyone made a puppet for the puppet show.

*Check your answers on page 117.*

## ON THE JOB

The two girls were arguing loudly. Then, Marcus came up to them. "What's all the fuss?" he asked.

"We want to know what you think," Jessica said. "Who's the better player—Chantelle or Annie?"

"Well, Chantelle is a terrific hitter, and Annie is a great fielder," Marcus answered. "But what's really important is that they are both team players. We're here to learn the game and have a good time, after all."

Marcus is an assistant coach in the after-school program at a neighborhood youth center. His job is to greet the boys and girls, make sure they get to their groups, and help with any problems.

Marcus is in charge of weight training, too. He helps teenagers set exercise goals and learn how to use the equipment. Marcus thinks that helping young people get into good shape is important.

Besides performing all of his other duties, Marcus acts as referee during the youth group soccer games. He makes sure that the equipment is in good shape. He also reminds players to wear safety gear.

On his job, Marcus must read different materials. He has to read team rosters and schedules. In the office there are books that give official rules for soccer and other games. Posters in the gym list instructions for the safe use of weights and other equipment. Marcus has a rule of his own: Make it fun, but keep it safe.

### TALK ABOUT IT

1. Describe the information Marcus gets from rule books.

2. Explain why it is important to read instructions on equipment.

Many camps have handbooks that give the camp rules and safety rules. The director at Hawk's Crest Day Camp gave Robert a coach's handbook. Robert must read the book. One section lists questions that players often ask about basketball. It suggests answers for those questions. Read the handbook section below.

# Hawk's Crest Day Camp
## Questions Campers Ask About Basketball

**Question 1:** "Why do you always tell me to pass the ball? I feel like I never get to shoot."

**Answer:** Knowing when to pass and when to shoot is an important skill. It is my job as coach to teach you this skill. If the team plays well together, everyone gets a chance to shoot.

**Question 2:** "Why do I have such a bad jump shot?"

**Answer:** When you are young, your leg muscles and other muscles are not yet fully developed. Therefore, you may have trouble with your jump shot. It is best not to push yourself to take jump shots if you are not ready.

**Question 3:** "Is it good to play through the pain if I get hurt?"

**Answer:** No. Playing injured is not smart . Playing injured can lead to more injury. Stop playing at once. Tell your coach if you are hurt or dizzy.

**Question 4:** "Why don't I get to play as much as the other players?"

**Answer:** It may seem as though other players are playing more. However, our goal is to give everyone fair playing time. I am watching the clock to make sure everyone gets enough time.

**Question 5:** "I'm such a bad player. How could I miss that shot?"

**Answer:** Missing a shot doesn't make you a bad player. Everyone misses a shot sometimes. Feeling bad won't improve your game. Just keep practicing, and you'll do your best.

**Question 6:** "I'm the star player. Why can't I get more playing time?"

**Answer:** Basketball is a team sport. No matter how good you are, you can't win the game alone. The goal is for everyone to learn to play as a team.

12                    *Hawk's Crest Day Camp*

# CHECK YOUR UNDERSTANDING

Answer each question based on the handbook on page 51.

1. Which statement tells a fact?

    a. It is my job as coach to teach you basketball skills.
    b. Knowing when to pass and when to shoot is an important skill.

2. Which statement tells a fact?

    a. When you are young, your leg muscles and other muscles are not yet fully developed.
    b. It is best not to push yourself to take jump shots if you are not ready.

3. Which statement gives an opinion?

    a. Playing injured is not smart.
    b. Playing injured can lead to more injury.

4. Which statement gives an opinion?

    a. I am watching the clock to make sure everyone gets enough time.
    b. It may seem as though other players are playing more.

For each fact that is stated below, give an opinion of your own. Write the opinion in the space provided.

**Example**

**Fact:** Our goal is to give everyone fair playing time.

**Opinion:** Giving everyone fair playing time is more important than winning every game.

5. **Fact:** Basketball is a team sport.
**Opinion:**


6. **Fact:** The goal is for everyone to learn to play as a team.
**Opinion:**


*Check your answers on page 117.*

## ◆ LESSON WRAP-UP

*Facts* are bits of information that can be proven to be true. *Opinions* are beliefs. Different people can have different opinions about the same facts. When you know the facts, you can decide whether or not to agree with a person's opinion.

We read about facts and opinions in everyday life. Newspapers, magazines, and books are major sources of facts and opinions.

**1.** Think about a subject of interest to you. The subject could be anything: education, parenting, crime, labor unions.

Write a short paragraph about the subject you choose. Include one or two facts as well as an opinion you have on the subject.

**2.** Facts on the job can involve dates, times, places, numbers, names, or procedures. For example, one fact may be that a job starts at 8 A.M. and ends at 4 P.M.

List three facts that you might be able to state about a job or the company where you work.

*Check your answers on page 117.*

# ◆ UNIT TWO REVIEW

**1.** List four steps to use in following written directions in lists and paragraphs. Briefly explain each step.

Step 1:

Step 2:

Step 3:

Step 4:

**2.** List three steps to use in following a schedule or agenda. Give an example for each step.

Step 1:

Step 2:

Step 3:

**3.** The following table gives some facts and some opinions. For every fact that is given, write an opinion. For every opinion that is given, write a fact. The first one is done as an example.

| Fact | Opinion |
|---|---|
| a. Elections are held on the first Tuesday in November. | a. There aren't any candidates worth voting for. |
| b. | b. She says she has the best job. |
| c. The restaurant serves Italian food. | c. |
| d. | d. He is the best coach in the program. |
| e. More children signed up for the camp this year than last year. | e. |
| f. | f. The classroom assistant seems to love working with children. |

*Check your answers on page 117.*

# Unit Three

## Hotel and Restaurant Jobs

Workers use many skills on the job. Cooks and chefs prepare food for customers. A hotel clerk greets guests, makes reservations, and accepts payment for rooms. A cashier works a cash register in a restaurant or other place. A food server takes orders and serves food in restaurants and coffee shops.

As in all industries, reading skills are important in hotel and restaurant work. In this unit, you will see how workers use these skills. A cook has to classify food items to figure out what can be made that week. A hotel clerk has to compare prices for rooms and services. A cashier must understand a memo explaining how carelessness causes loss of money. A food server looks at instructions for causes and effects when using a machine on the job.

This unit teaches the following reading skills:

- ◆ classifying information
- ◆ comparing and contrasting
- ◆ identifying cause and effect by asking questions
- ◆ identifying cause and effect by looking for clue words

You will learn how workers in the hotel and restaurant industries use these reading skills in their work.

# Preparing Foods

Preparing food for people is big business. There are many different restaurants serving many kinds of food. Fast-food restaurants, coffee shops, and table-service restaurants are some popular ones.

In every restaurant, the quality of the food is very important. Customers want a good meal at the right price. Restaurant owners hire cooks and chefs to make food that customers will enjoy.

Chefs and cooks need to be organized in order to quickly prepare many meals. Classifying, or grouping, the materials they use is important to them.

**Classifying information** is an important skill in reading, too. Knowing how information is arranged makes the information easier to understand.

## *Job Focus*

There are many types of **cooks.** Fancy restaurants often hire highly skilled cooks, or chefs, to run the kitchen. Some cooks work in schools, hospitals, and similar places. Short-order cooks work in coffee shops and other restaurants that provide fast service.

Kitchen work is fast-paced. Often, the kitchen is hot, noisy, and messy. Food preparers must be able to stand on their feet for long periods of time. They must be able to lift heavy pots and work in a crowded space. It is important for cooks to be able to work as a team. They should also have a good sense of taste and smell.

There are more than 3.2 million jobs held by chefs, cooks, and other kitchen workers. Many job openings are expected through the year 2005. Jobs in table-service restaurants may grow more quickly than jobs in fast-food restaurants.

# Classifying Information: How It Works

**Classifying information** is the skill of organizing items of information into groups. The items in a group are alike in some way.

A good way to organize information into groups, or categories, is to use a table. A table gives information clearly in a small amount of space. Look at the table on this page as you read the following.

**Table Title:** A title tells what the table is about. The title of this table is "Ice Cream and Fruit Sundaes."

**Columns and Rows:** A table has columns and rows. Columns run up and down. Rows run from left to right.

**Column Headings:** At the top of each column is a heading. The heading names the category. The column headings in this table are "Strawberry Surprise," "Banana Split," and "Peach Delight."

**Row Headings:** A row can have a heading, too. Row headings appear at the left of the table. The row headings here are "Fruit," "Ice cream," and "Topping."

## Ice Cream and Fruit Sundaes

|  | Strawberry Surprise | Banana Split | Peach Delight |
|---|---|---|---|
| Fruit | 1/2 cup | 1 banana | 1/2 cup |
| Ice cream | 2 scoops | 3 scoops | 2 scoops |
| Topping | Whipped cream, Syrup | Whipped cream, Syrup, Nuts | Whipped cream, Syrup |

An item in a table falls into two categories. To read a table, find the row and column headings you need. Then, find where the row and the column meet to find the item that refers to both categories.

Use the table to answer this question: How much ice cream is in the Peach Delight?

---

Find the row heading marked "Ice cream." Follow the row to the column with the heading "Peach Delight." The place where the row and the column meet gives you the answer. *Peach Delight has two scoops of ice cream.*

**ingredients**
(ihn-GREE-dee-ehnts) things combined together to make a food

**inventory**
(IHN-vehn-tawr-ee) a count of goods and materials in stock

Carlos is a pie maker. It is his job to bake pies and pastries every day at work. Every week he meets with the chef, who tells him what to bake. The chef is the head cook—the person in charge of the restaurant kitchen.

Carlos uses prepared **ingredients** to make his baked goods. He helps the manager take an **inventory** of ingredients. From the inventory and the chef's orders, Carlos and the manager figure out what ingredients are needed for the week.

Shown here are a table with the chef's orders and the inventory list for the week.

| Baked Goods Orders for the Week of May 20 | | | | | |
|---|---|---|---|---|---|
| | **MONDAY** | **TUESDAY** | **WEDNESDAY** | **THURSDAY** | **FRIDAY** |
| Sugar buns | 6 | 6 | 10 | 6 | 4 |
| Cheese Danish | 6 | 6 | 8 | 6 | 4 |
| Fruit Danish | 12 | 12 | 12 | 12 | 8 |
| Bagels | 12 | 12 | 18 | 12 | 8 |
| Blueberry pies | 1 | 1 | 1 | 1 | 1 |
| Apple pies | 1 | 1 | 2 | 1 | 1 |
| Special | 1 peach pie | 1 strawberry rhubarb pie | 1 chocolate cream pie | 1 Dutch apple pie | 1 raspberry tart |

**INVENTORY—BAKED GOODS**

| | |
|---|---|
| **Week of** | May 20 |
| Frozen pie crusts | 2 |
| Frozen Danish pastry sheets | 6 |
| Frozen sugar buns | 1 dozen |
| Sugar bun topping | 0 |
| Danish cheese filling | 1 package |
| Danish fruit filling | 1 can |
| Apple pie filling | 2 cans |
| Blueberry pie filling | $1\frac{1}{2}$ cans |
| Other: peach filling | 1 can |

**LESSON 8 ◆ PREPARING FOODS**

Answer each question based on the table and the list on page 58.

1. List the column headings used in the table.

2. List the row headings used in the table.

3. What time period does the menu cover?

4. How many kinds of filling are listed on the inventory list? What are they?

5. How many kinds of frozen items are listed on the inventory list? What are they?

Circle the letter of the correct answer.

6. For which day must Carlos bake the most sugar buns?
   a. Wednesday
   b. Thursday
   c. Friday

7. How many bagels must Carlos bake for the entire week?
   a. 8
   b. 18
   c. 62

8. For which day must Carlos bake two different kinds of apple pie?
   a. Monday
   b. every day
   c. Thursday

**9.** It takes one frozen pie crust to make a pie. How many frozen pie crusts must Carlos order for the week?

**10.** It takes half a can of filling to make one pie. How much blueberry filling must Carlos order for the week?

*Check your answers on page 118.*

## ON THE JOB

Felipe enjoys his job. He gets to meet people, cook good food, and show off his talents. Felipe works as a specialty cook in a pizzeria, or pizza shop. A *specialty cook* makes one type of food.

The pizzeria is located in a shopping mall. Felipe works behind a large window. He shapes the pizza dough, tossing it into the air and catching it to stretch the dough. Customers love to watch Felipe handle the dough.

Carefully and smoothly, Felipe puts toppings on the pizza dough. First, he puts on tomato sauce. Then, he adds grated cheeses. Next, he sprinkles on oil and spices. Sometimes, he adds other toppings, too. Finally, the pizza is ready for baking.

Felipe's job includes behind-the-scenes work, too. He must read ingredient labels and instructions, as well as prepare and measure the ingredients. He must write down take-out orders. Felipe also needs to read notices from his boss. However, his favorite part of the job is watching customers smile as he tosses the dough high above his head and catches it.

### TALK ABOUT IT
**1.** Name two items that Felipe must be able to read.

**2.** Discuss whether this would be a good job for someone who does not like to work with the public.

**garnishes** (GAHR-nihsh-ehz) food used as decoration, like parsley or a slice of fruit

The Milton Cafe is a coffee shop on the main street of a small town. Danielle works at the cafe as a salad person. She prepares salad materials. She puts salads and **garnishes** on plates of food. She also works as a general helper and dishwasher.

Danielle works with the cook. When the cook finishes cooking a meal, he hands the plate of food to Danielle. She looks at a table. The table tells her which side dishes, salads, and garnishes belong on the dish. Danielle arranges the food on plates. Then, she puts the completed dishes out for the server.

**menu** (MEHN-yoo) a list of foods that may be ordered in a restaurant

Look at the table of **menu** items that Danielle uses.

## Milton Cafe — SALADS AND SIDE ORDERS

| MENU ITEM | SIDE DISHES | GARNISH | SALAD | BREAD |
|---|---|---|---|---|
| Hamburger | None | 1/4 pickle<br>Cole slaw cup | None | Bun |
| Hamburger Deluxe | 10 French fries<br>Lettuce<br>2 tomato slices | 1/4 pickle<br>Cole slaw cup | None | Bun |
| Grilled Chicken Platter | Salad AND<br>1/2 cup rice OR<br>10 French fries | 1/4 pickle<br>Lemon wedge | Yes | Roll & butter |
| Fried Fish Platter | Salad AND<br>1/2 cup rice OR<br>10 French fries | Lemon wedge<br>Tartar sauce cup | Yes | Roll & butter |
| Vegetarian Chili | Salad AND<br>1/2 cup rice | 1 tablespoon grated cheddar<br>Sour cream cup | Yes | Roll & butter |

Answer each question based on the table on page 61.

1. List the categories shown in the column headings.

2. List the categories shown in the row headings.

3. What items belong in the category labeled "Garnish"?

4. Which category contains no side dishes?

5. How many categories contain salad as a side dish?

6. Find the box in which Garnish and Grilled Chicken Platter meet. Write a sentence that tells the information in the box.

7. Find the category "Vegetarian Chili." Describe all of the extras that come with an order of vegetarian chili.

8. The restaurant owner is adding an item to the menu. Read the menu description given here. Then, fill in the table that follows. Use the table on page 61 as your guide.

**Roast Turkey Platter:** Slices of white meat turkey. Served with rice, cranberry sauce garnish, and salad with dressing. Roll and butter included.

| MENU ITEM | SIDE DISHES | GARNISH | SALAD | BREAD |
|-----------|-------------|---------|-------|-------|
|           |             |         |       |       |

*Check your answers on page 118.*

## ◆ LESSON WRAP-UP

Classifying items into groups is a way of organizing information. It helps you get the most from the information you read. Each group contains items that are alike in some way.

Tables contain information grouped by categories. The categories are shown by the column and row headings. To read a table, find the row and column headings of the categories that interest you. Find where the row and the column meet. This process will lead you to information that both categories have in common.

1. We use tables at work and in everyday life. For example, many brands of pancake mix have a table on the back of the box. The table shows different amounts of ingredients for different numbers of pancakes.

Look for tables on food boxes, in newspapers, in instruction booklets, on catalog order sheets, and in other places. Choose one table. Tell why you think that the information was put in table form instead of paragraph form.

2. The headings in the telephone *Yellow Pages* list different categories. Suppose you want to buy or adopt a pet. You might look in the *Yellow Pages* under the following headings: Pet Shops, Animal Shelters, and Animal Organizations.

Choose one of the following topics: Summer programs for children; prenatal care; long-distance travel. What categories would you look under in the Yellow Pages for information about the topic?

*Check your answers on page 118.*

# Taking Care of Guests

▼▼▼▼▼▼▼▼▼▼▼▼
**Words to Know**

complimentary

continental breakfast

double occupancy

single occupancy

suites

terrace

When people travel, they may need a place to stay. Travelers might stay in a small inn with only a few rooms and a homelike setting. They may stay in a motel that has a restaurant and parking. They may stay in a large hotel that offers a pool, a gym, room service, and several places to eat.

Inns, motels, hotels—all these places need service workers. It is their job to make a guest's stay pleasant.

The hotel clerk may be the first hotel worker that a guest meets. The clerk may have to look at room rates, menus, and other items to give the guest information. He or she may have to compare the costs or features of different items for a guest.

*Comparing* items involves finding out how the items are alike. *Contrasting* items involves finding out how they are different. Both are important reading skills. By **comparing and contrasting** information, the hotel clerk can help guests make choices and decisions.

## Job Focus

**Hotel clerks** greet guests when they arrive. Clerks assign rooms and keep records of guest expenses. Hotel clerks may also make reservations and collect room fees when guests check out.

Hotel clerks need to be polite and patient at all times. They often explain hotel costs to guests who have questions about their bills. Hotel clerks must have good speaking and listening skills.

More than 100,000 workers have jobs as hotel clerks. The number of these jobs will grow through the year 2005. Promotions in hotels also will make room for new clerks to be hired.

# Comparing and Contrasting: How It Works

One way writers give information is to **compare and contrast** ideas or things. In *comparing* items, a writer tells how the items are alike. In *contrasting* items, the writer tells how the items are different. Writers use two methods to compare and contrast.

**Method 1: Point-by-Point Comparison.** The writer compares and contrasts each feature, or "point," of the things being compared. Read the following point-by-point comparison from a hotel brochure.

suites (sweets) hotel units with more than one room (in addition to the bathroom)

terrace (TAIR-ehs) patio

> The Lincoln **Suite** and the Washington Suite both feature a bedroom and a sitting room. Each has a large whirlpool bath. The Lincoln Suite also offers a private **terrace** with a view of the park. The Washington Suite opens onto our award-winning garden patio.

The paragraph compares the two suites on three points: rooms, baths, and extra features (terrace and patio). On which two points are the suites alike?

_____

*Both have the same types of rooms and bath.*

**Method 2: Alternating Descriptions.** First, the author writes all about one item. Then, the author writes all about the other item. The following paragraphs from a hotel brochure use alternating descriptions.

> Make yourself at home in our beautiful Lincoln Suite, which features a luxurious bedroom and sitting room, as well as a large whirlpool bath. Enjoy breakfast on your own private terrace with a view of the park.
>
> Relax in our delightful Washington Suite. A large whirlpool bath comes with a luxurious bedroom and sitting room. Step out onto our award-winning garden patio from your own private entrance.

The first paragraph is about the Lincoln Suite only. The second paragraph is about the Washington Suite only. In what way are the two suites different?

_____

*Lincoln Suite has a private terrace; Washington Suite has a private entrance to the garden patio.*

**R**aymond works as a hotel clerk. He is in charge of reservations. Part of his job is to send letters to possible guests. The manager has given Raymond two sample letters to study. Look at the following letters.

**Letter 1**

> Boulevard Hotel
> Maine Boulevard at Elm Street
> Hope, Pennsylvania
>
> Dear Manager,
>
> Please send information on your room rates. We will be in Hope for a wedding the weekend of June 4 to 6. We will need rooms for 20 adults and 5 children.
>
> Also, please let me know if there is a restaurant nearby.
>
> Sincerely,
> Alfred Guest

**Letter 2**

> Boulevard Hotel
> Maine Boulevard at Elm Street
> Hope, Pennsylvania
>
> Dear Mr. Guest,
>
> Thank you for your request for information.
>
> We can provide ten double rooms at $55 a night per person. Two adults can share a double room. Single rooms are available at $75 a night per person.
>
> Children under ten stay in their parents' room free of charge. Children between ten and eighteen stay in their parents' room at half price.
>
> We offer a **complimentary continental breakfast** of coffee or tea and a sweet roll in our lounge between 7 and 10 in the morning. There is no restaurant in the hotel; however, there are two coffee shops within walking distance.
>
> We look forward to serving you. Please do not hesitate to call with any questions.
>
> Sincerely,
> Manager

**complimentary**
(kahm-pluh-MEHN-tuh-ree)
free of charge

**continental breakfast**
(kahn-tih-NEHNT-uhl brehk-fehst) a light morning snack

**LESSON 9 ◆ TAKING CARE OF GUESTS**

# CHECK YOUR UNDERSTANDING

Answer each question based on the letters on page 66.

1. Double rooms cost
   a. $55.00 a night a room.
   b. $55.00 a person a night.
   c. $75.00 a room.

2. A double room may *not* be shared by
   a. parents and children.
   b. two adults.
   c. three adults.

3. Food may be purchased at
   a. a restaurant in the hotel.
   b. a coffee shop next door to the hotel.
   c. two coffee shops within walking distance of the hotel.

4. Why is Mr. Guest traveling to Hope?


5. How many nights will Mr. Guest stay at the hotel? What are the dates?



6. Compare the price of a double room and a single room. Which costs more per person?



7. Compare the rates for children under ten with the rates for children over ten. Which rates are higher?



Underline **True** if a statement is true. Underline **False** if it is false.

True   False      8. A guest can order dinner at the hotel.

True   False      9. A guest can get free coffee in the morning.

True   False      10. A guest can walk to a coffee shop from the hotel.

*Check your answers on page 118.*

The snow had just begun to fall. It was going to be a beautiful winter season. Melissa liked this time of year at work. The hotel was busier than at other times. It hummed with activity.

Melissa works as a hotel clerk in a medium-sized hotel. She greets guests when they arrive and checks their reservations. Then, she selects a room and gives them their room key.

Guests arrive from all over the country and all over the world. Weekday guests are often business travelers. Weekend guests are usually tourists on vacation.

Sometimes, guests need special information. They might want to know about hotel services. They might want to know about tourist services. They might want to schedule a wake-up call.

Melissa tries to give information cheerfully and promptly. She looks at brochures, price charts, telephone books, and other materials. She even arranges for morning wake-up calls.

When guests are ready to leave, Melissa checks them out of the hotel. She makes sure their bill is correct. She collects the payment as well as the room key.

The hotel desk is open 24 hours a day. This means that Melissa sometimes has to work the night shift. Still, Melissa really likes her job. She meets all kinds of interesting people. She likes the excitement and activity. Melissa plans to take some business courses. She wants to work her way up to management.

## TALK ABOUT IT

1. Describe the materials that Melissa reads to get information for guests.

2. Discuss the career plans that Melissa has.

3. Tell about the kinds of people that Melissa meets.

**single occupancy**
(AHK-yoo-pehn-see) rental of a hotel room by one person

**double occupancy** rental of a hotel room by two people

The Star Hotel has different rooms available. Some rooms are big or have special features. The prices vary depending on the type of room.

Prices also vary with the season. During the busy season, prices for all rooms are higher.

Look at the price list given here. The hotel clerk makes reservations for guests using this list.

## STAR HOTEL    Price List

### Per Person/Per Night

| UNIT | Nov. 1-April 30 | | May 1-Oct. 31 | |
|------|------|------|------|------|
| | *Weekdays* | *Weekends* | *Weekdays* | *Weekends* |
| Single room | $50 | $55 | $40 | $45 |
| Double room:<br>    Single occupancy<br>    Double occupancy | $70<br>$45 | $75<br>$50 | $60<br>$35 | $65<br>$40 |
| Terrace suite | $90 | $95 | $80 | $85 |
| Poolside suite | $100 | $105 | $90 | $95 |
| Children under 12 | $15 | $15 | $15 | $15 |

*Additional Information*

✶ All rooms have private baths.

✶ Single rooms have one double bed.

✶ Double rooms have two double beds.

✶ A portable bed is provided for children under 12 staying in the same room with one or two parents.

✶ Cribs are provided free of charge for infants.

✶ Weekdays are Monday night through Thursday night.

✶ Weekends are Friday night through Sunday night.

## CHECK YOUR UNDERSTANDING

Answer each question based on the price list above.

I. Which is the least expensive unit available for December 5?

    a. single room

    b. double room

    c. suite

**2.** Which is the most expensive unit available for June 15?

   a. double room

   b. poolside suite

   c. terrace suite

**3.** When are the rooms more expensive?

   a. weekdays

   b. May 1-October 31

   c. weekends

**4.** Which units have lower rates in June than in February?

   a. double rooms only

   b. terrace suite only

   c. all units

Using the price list, figure out the different costs for each guest. Then, compare the costs.

**Example:** Ricky wants to rent a double room for two weekend nights. He cannot decide whether to rent in August or October.

   a. Find the cost of a double room, single occupancy, for one weekend night in August: $65

   b. Find the cost of a double room, single occupancy, for one weekend night in October: $65

   c. Compare costs in *a* and *b* above. The costs are the same.

**5.** Two friends need a hotel room to stay overnight on a weekday in June. They want to know the rates for different rooms.

   a. Find the rate for a single room for one night:

   b. Multiply the cost in *a* by 2 for two people: _____ x 2 = _____.

   c. Find the rate for a double room, double occupancy, for one night:

   d. Multiply the cost in *c* by 2 for two people: _____ x 2 = _____.

   e. Compare the cost in *b* (two single rooms) and the cost in *d* (one double room occupied by two people).

*Check your answers on page 119.*

**LESSON 9 ◆ TAKING CARE OF GUESTS**

## ◆ LESSON WRAP-UP

Comparing and contrasting is one way writers give information. To recognize comparing and contrasting, look for these patterns:

**Point-by-point comparison.** The writer compares the two items one point at a time.

**Alternating descriptions.** The writer explains all the points about one item. Then, the writer explains all the points about the second item.

Comparing items helps us make decisions. By thinking about each point, we discover which item is better for us.

1. Find two similar written items to compare. You can use newspaper ads for jobs or apartments or cars. Write a point-by-point comparison of the two items, using at least three points.

2. Comparing and contrasting can help you find the kind of job that is better for you. Think of your likes and dislikes. Now, think about jobs characteristics that fit your likes and dislikes. Fill in the chart given here. Add two more job characteristics, and show whether you like or dislike them.

| Job Characteristic | Like | Dislike |
|---|---|---|
| Working with customers | | |
| Working with children | | |
| Working with machinery | | |
| Dressing formally | | |
| Dressing informally | | |
| Working indoors | | |
| Working outdoors | | |

*Check your answers on page 119.*

# Working at a Cash Register

Many service jobs involve taking money and making change. A person who does this job may be called a *cashier* (ka-SHEER) or a *checker*. A cashier or checker uses a cash register to record payments, store cash, and make change.

A worker who handles money has an important job. He or she must be fast yet make very few mistakes. A cashier who does not make the proper change hurts a business. Mistakes cause too much or too little money to be in the cash register at the end of the day. Too much money means that customers have been cheated. Too little money means that the business has lost money.

**Identifying cause and effect** is very important in working with money. It also is an important reading skill for cashiers. You will use this skill in this lesson when you read workplace materials that cashiers read.

## Job Focus

**Cashiers** and **checkers** handle payments made with cash, credit cards, and checks. They work with keypads, computer screens, scanners, and credit card readers. They count their money supply at the beginning and end of each shift.

To work as a cashier or checker, you must like working with numbers. Because checkers and cashiers also work with customers, they must be polite and make as few mistakes as possible.

Working a cash register can start a career. Cashiers now hold about 3 million jobs. Many of these workers get promoted to better jobs where they work.

# Identifying Cause and Effect: How It Works

"What will happen if I take this action?" When we ask a question like this, we want to know about causes and effects.

A *cause* is what makes something happen. An *effect* is what happens. **Identifying cause and effect** means figuring out which cause produces which effect.

A worker should be able to identify cause and effect on the job. This reading skill can help the worker understand why a method should be used. With this skill, a worker also can explain how to prevent mistakes.

Read the guidelines for the **cash register** drawer below.

**cash register**

(kash REJ-ihs-ter) a machine that records sales, stores cash from sales, and gives receipts

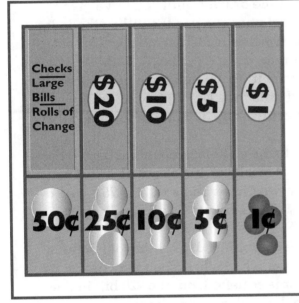

**Guidelines for Arrangement of the Cash Register Drawer**

All cash drawers must be arranged as shown for these reasons:

1. Most checkers in all jobs use this arrangement.
2. If all drawers are set up the same way, there are fewer mistakes.
3. It is easy to remember the positions of the bills and coins. The compartments that go together have one digit in common. For example, the $5 bills are behind the $.05 coins (nickels), and both have the digit "5."

To find the effect, ask, "What happened? What is the result?" For example, look at guideline 2. What is the effect of all drawers being set up the same way?

*There are fewer mistakes.*

To find the cause, ask, "Why did this happen? What action produced this result?" For example, look at guideline 3. The effect is "It is easy to remember the positions of the bills and coins." What action produced this effect?

*Putting together compartments that have one digit in common.*

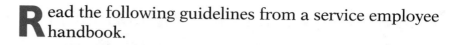

Read the following guidelines from a service employee handbook.

---

### Guidelines for Cash Register Cashiers: Making Change

Cashiers who follow these guidelines have fewer arguments with customers about payments and change.

1. After entering the sale, tell the customer the total amount. For example, say, "The total is $15.55, including the tax."
2. Say aloud the amount that the customer gives you. Use a phrase like "Out of $20." When the customer hears the amount, the customer is less likely to argue later.
3. Do not put the money in the drawer. Leave the money on the ledge above the drawer until you have given the change. The customer can see the bill on the ledge. Therefore, the customer is less likely to argue about the **amount tendered**.
4. Count up the change from the purchase price. Use smaller coins and bills first. Use as few coins as possible. Customers usually do not like to get too many coins.
5. Hand the change to the customer, counting aloud. For example, say, "That total was $15.55 out of $20." Then give the customer two dimes and say, "$15.75"; then a quarter and say "$16"; then four $1 bills and say, "$17, $18, $19, and $20."
6. If the customer seems confused, explain your actions patiently. A customer who feels rushed may get angry.
7. Once the customer is satisfied, put the $20 bill in the drawer and close the cash register drawer.

*Guidelines*                                              *35*

---

**amount tendered**
(uh-MOWNT TEHN-derd)
money given as payment

---

## CHECK YOUR UNDERSTANDING

Answer each question based on the guidelines. For every cause given, write the correct effect.

**Example: Cause:** The cashiers follow these guidelines.
**Effect:** The cashiers have fewer arguments with customers over payments and change.

1. **Cause:** The customer hears the amount.
**Effect:**

**2. Cause:** Customers usually do not like to get too many coins.
**Effect:**

**3. Cause:** The customer feels rushed.
**Effect:**

For every effect given, write the correct cause.

**4. Effect:** Explain your actions patiently.
**Cause:**

**5. Effect:** Put the $20 bill in the drawer, and close the cash-register drawer.
**Cause:**

**6. Effect:** The customer will be less likely to argue about the amount tendered.
**Cause:**

*Check your answers on page 119.*

## ON THE JOB

Bill has a job as a cashier in a museum cafeteria. Bill likes working with numbers. He also enjoys working in the museum. The crowds of visitors are interesting. People are usually in a good mood.

Bill's day begins at 11:00 A.M., when the cafeteria opens. Bill gets his cash drawer from his supervisor. He checks that the amount of money in the drawer matches the amount that should be there. He counts the number of $1 bills, $5 bills, and $10 bills. He counts all the coins. Everything has to be counted.

On his job, Bill had to learn the keys on his cash register. He also reads the menu every day to learn the special meals and their prices.

At the end of the day, Bill balances the cash. He counts the money in the drawer. The amount must match the figure on the cash-register tape. Then, he fills out a short report. The report lists the beginning amount and the ending amount for the day.

### TALK ABOUT IT
1. Discuss why Bill finds his job interesting.

2. Describe why Bill reads the menu every day.

**IDENTIFYING CAUSE AND EFFECT**

R ead the memo below about safety when handling cash.

**memo** (MEHM-oh) a written message sent within a company

**transactions** (tran-ZAKT-shunz) exchanges of payments for purchases between customers and a store

**balancing** (BAL-ehns-ihng) **the cash** accounting for the day's sales and money

**over** more cash than the amount recorded on the cash-register tape

**short** less cash than the amount recorded on the cash-register tape

**even** (EE-vehn) the same amount of cash in the drawer as recorded on the cash-register tape

---

# M E M O

TO: All Cashiers
FROM: Management
DATE: September 21
SUBJECT: Safety Rules

Recently, there have been a few problems with losses of cash. If we all remember to follow the safety rules, we will have fewer cash losses.

Cashiers should keep the cash drawer closed between **transactions.** If a cash drawer is open, money can easily be taken.

A customer may interrupt you with a question while you are counting change. Ignore the interruption and continue counting. When you are done, you can politely answer the customer.

Pay extra attention when you are **balancing the cash.** If your cash drawer is **over**, you have taken in too much money or given too little in change. If the drawer is **short**, you have given too much in change or taken too little in payment. Let the manager know immediately. If your cash drawer is **even**, good work!

---

## CHECK YOUR UNDERSTANDING

For each cause, circle the letter of the effect given in the memo.

**1.** If all cashiers remember to follow the safety rules,
    a. they will get a better job.
    b. they will have fewer losses of cash.
    c. they should all have more money.

**2.** If a cash-register drawer is kept open,
    a. it's alright because that makes it easier for the cashier to work.
    b. it means the cashier is very busy.
    c. it is easier for money to be stolen.

**3.** If your drawer is over or short,
    a. let your manager know.
    b. fix the cash register.
    c. report a theft.

Complete each effect by writing *over, short,* or *even* in the space provided.

4. **Cause:** The cashier pays out too much in change.
**Effect:** The cash drawer will be

5. **Cause:** The cashier pays out too little in change.
**Effect:** The cash drawer will be

6. **Cause:** The cashier takes in too little in payment.
**Effect:** The cash drawer will be

7. **Cause:** The cashier makes the right change every time.
**Effect:** The cash drawer will be

8. Read these cause-and-effect statements. Which one accurately expresses the main idea of the memo?
   a. Interruptions by customers cause losses of cash.
   b. Careless handling of money causes losses of cash.
   c. Broken cash registers cause losses of cash.

*Check your answers on page 119.*

## ◆ LESSON WRAP-UP

In a cause-and-effect relationship, the cause produces the effect. To find the cause, we ask questions like "What happened?" To find the effect, we ask questions like "What is the result?"

In everyday life, we deal with cause and effect all the time. A broken-down bus may cause us to be late for work. An illness may cause us to stay home in bed. An argument with a spouse may cause us to be unhappy.

Write an effect for each cause given below.

1. **Cause:** a traffic accident on the highway
**Effect:**

2. **Cause:** heavy traffic on the highway
**Effect:**

3. **Cause:** only two cashiers working in a busy store
**Effect:**

*Check your answers on page 119.*

# Serving Food

▼▼▼▼▼▼▼▼▼▼▼

**Words to Know**

Heimlich maneuver

hygiene

setup

utensils

One important job in the restaurant business is that of waiting on customers. Food servers (waiters and waitresses) do many tasks. They take customer orders and give the orders to the kitchen. When the food is ready, servers bring the food to the table.

Restaurants depend heavily on the skill of their servers. Customers may complain about slow service or bad-tempered servers. Poor service can cause a loss of business for restaurants. A server needs to know the effects of his or her actions.

The server also needs to **identify causes and effects** in writing. Finding clue words helps the server understand written materials on the job.

## Job Focus

**Food service workers** must be able to work well under pressure. They must carry heavy trays of dishes and glassware. They are on their feet for long hours.

At the same time, food service workers must be polite and helpful to customers. They must know the menu well. They must remain calm even when customers are difficult.

At fine restaurants, food servers may offer more personal service. They may suggest a wine for a certain dish. They may explain how a dish is prepared.

In coffee shops, food servers may set and clear tables and seat guests. They may serve meals at the counter. They may make fountain drinks, salads, and desserts.

At fast-food restaurants, servers ring up orders at a cash register. They get the ordered foods and package them. They also may prepare drinks and some foods.

Food service workers hold more than 3 million jobs. There are many job openings expected through the year 2005.

# Identifying Cause and Effect: How It Works

Writers often use clue words. A clue word tells you the relationship between actions or ideas. For example, think about the clue words *first, next,* and *last.* What do they tell you? They tell you the order among three actions. One happened first, one happened second, and one happened last.

Some clue words tell the reader to watch for cause-and-effect relationships. Perhaps the most common one is *because.* (Notice that *because* has the word *cause* in it.) Sometimes, words are put together to form a clue—like *because of.* Some common clue words for *cause* are *because, because of, since,* and *if.* Some common clue words for *effect* are *as a result, as a result of, consequently, as a consequence, so, so that, then,* and *therefore.*

The word *since* can be a cause-and-effect clue when it is used to mean *because;* for example, "Since the pay is good, I will stay with the job."

Looking for clue words will help you spot cause-and-effect relationships.

Read the safety tips given here.

**hygiene** (HY-jeen) conditions, such as cleanliness, that are good for health

## HYGIENE AND SAFETY TIPS

1. Servers should always wear a clean uniform since looking clean and neat makes a good impression on customers.
2. Servers should always wash hands after using the toilet because dirty hands spread disease.
3. Servers should always keep long hair pinned up and neat so that it does not get into food.
4. Servers should learn the **Heimlich maneuver.** As a result, they may one day save a life.

**Heimlich maneuver** (HEYEM-lik muh-NOO-ver) an emergency technique to help choking victims

Underline the clue words in the Hygiene and Safety Tips.

Did you find *since, because, so that,* and *as a result?*

When you find clue words, ask yourself if they come before a cause or an effect. In tip 1, what cause does the word *since* come before?

_____

*Looking clean and neat makes a good impression on customers.* What is the effect of this cause?

_____

*Servers should always wear a clean uniform.*

ome restaurants may have a list of procedures to
follow when setting up a dining room.

**setup** (SEHT-up) preparation
of a dining room for business

**utensils** (yoo-TEHN-sihlz)
items, such as knives, forks,
and spoons, used for eating
or cooking

---

**SETUP** PROCEDURES

Set up all tables before closing <u>so that</u> tables are
ready right away in the morning.

1. Since it may be hard to tell if a table is dirty,
   wipe down all table tops.
2. Put a paper placemat at each serving place
   because placemats make cleanup easier.
3. Put a napkin at the left on the placemat.
4. Arrange **utensils** as follows so that all settings
   look the same:
   a. Put a fork on the napkin.
   b. Put a knife on the right side of the
      placemat.
   c. Put a teaspoon to the right of the knife.
5. Place a water glass above the fork. If you turn
   the glass upside down, it will stay clean.
6. Place a saucer and coffee cup above the spoon.
   Turn the cup over; then it will stay clean.
7. Place the salt, pepper, and sugar bowl in the
   center of the table.

---

## CHECK YOUR UNDERSTANDING

Underline all the clue words in the reading. (See the list of clue
words on page 79.) Then, fill in the correct answer.

**Example:** Which clue word appears in the first sentence?
*so that*

1. Which clue word appears in item 1?

2. Which clue word appears in item 2?

3. Which clue word appears in item 4?

4. Which clue word appears in item 5?

**5.** Which clue word appears in item 6?

For every cause, write the effect described in the reading.

**Example:** What is the effect of setting up all the tables before closing?
The tables will be ready for customers first thing in the morning.

**6.** What is the effect of using paper placemats?

**7.** What is the effect of following one arrangement for utensils?

**8.** What is the effect of turning glasses upside down?

*Check your answers on page 119.*

## ON THE JOB

As a food server, Ronald works hard to satisfy his customers. He is learning all that he can because he plans to open his own restaurant one day.

It is part of Ronald's job to greet customers and show them to a table. After the guests are comfortable, he hands them menus. There are always several daily specials. Ronald has to tell customers the specials, since they are not listed on the menu.

Ronald takes orders, noting which guest ordered which dish. He often has to follow special directions. For example, some diners want salad dressing on the side or rice instead of potatoes.

Each day, Ronald reads and learns the list of specials. He looks at the menu for any price changes. He also reads memos, posters, and other items. Reading these materials is an important part of the job.

### TALK ABOUT IT
**1.** Discuss why reading is an important part of Ronald's job.

**2.** Describe Ronald's plans for the future.

**IDENTIFYING CAUSE AND EFFECT**

**A** server who works at a coffee shop counter needs to use equipment like coffee makers. The server may have to clean and assemble the equipment, too.

---

### ESPRESSO MACHINE INSTRUCTIONS

Since we have had many requests, we are now offering espresso and cappuccino. Please read the following instructions carefully. Injury can happen as a result of improper use of the equipment.

*To make espresso:*
1. Make sure the machine is off.
2. Insert the filter into the filter holder.
3. Fill the filter with ground espresso beans to the fill line.
4. Turn the filter holder handle to the right to lock the holder in place.
5. Fill water tank to the fill line.
6. Switch the machine on.

*Caution*
1. If the ground espresso beans are packed too tightly, the machine will not work properly.
2. Clogging or overflow may occur as a result of filling ground espresso beans above the fill line.
3. Wipe the steamer after each use so that it does not become clogged.
4. Use only cold water. Then, there is less risk of damage and injury.

---

## CHECK YOUR UNDERSTANDING

Underline all the clue words in the reading. (See the list of clue words on page 79.) Then, fill in the correct answer.

1. Which clue word appears in caution 1?

2. Which clue word appears in caution 2?

3. Which clue word appears in caution 3?

4. Which clue word appears in caution 4?

5. What is the effect of packing the ground espresso too tightly?

**6.** What is the effect of filling ground espresso beans above the fill line?

**7.** What is the effect of wiping the steamer after each use?

**8.** What is the effect of using only cold water?

In each sentence below, a clue word is underlined. Rewrite the sentence using a different clue word that has the same meaning. It's alright to move the new clue word to a different place in the sentence.

**Example:** <u>Since</u> we have had many requests, we are now offering espresso and cappuccino.

We have had many requests. As a result, we are now offering espresso and cappuccino.

**9.** The new server filled the filter too full. <u>Therefore,</u> the espresso machine overflowed.

**10.** Injury can happen as <u>a result of</u> improper use of the equipment.

*Check your answers on page 119.*

## ◆ LESSON WRAP-UP

Certain clue words tell you to watch for cause-and-effect relationships. We see these clue words in all kinds of writing. For example, instructions, memos, and newspaper stories may contain these words.

Clue words are used below. Write an ending for each item to turn it into a complete sentence.

**Example:** Since I quit smoking, I am not short of breath all of the time.

**1.** If you want a tax refund,

**2.** Because I get sick from milk,

**3.** As a result of working overtime,

*Check your answers on page 120.*

**IDENTIFYING CAUSE AND EFFECT**

# ◆ UNIT THREE REVIEW

**1.** Write a short paragraph giving a point-by-point comparison of the jobs of hotel clerk and food server. Compare at least three points, such as "works with the public."

**2.** In a short paragraph, write alternating descriptions of the pros (good points) and cons (bad points) of being a cashier.

**3.** Write two questions that you can ask to find the cause of each of the following situations.

   a. A machine accident happens at work.

   b. A restaurant goes out of business.

**4.** Write two questions that you can ask to find the effect of each of the following situations.

   a. A hotel clerk argued loudly with a guest.

   b. A cashier's cash register was short for three days in a row.

**5.** Use the following clue words in a sentence that shows cause and effect.

   a. because:

   b. if:

   c. so that:

*Check your answers on page 120.*

# · Retail Sales Jobs ·

Salespeople work with customers to make sales. Salesclerks give information and accept payments for items. Stock clerks receive, check, label, and shelve shipments of goods.

Reading skills are important for these jobs, as they are for jobs in other industries. In this unit, you will learn about some of the reading materials that are used in retail sales jobs. A salesperson draws conclusions from a magazine article about a selling method. A salesclerk gathers information from a sales check and a refund slip. A stock clerk draws conclusions from the floor plan of a stockroom.

This unit teaches the following reading skills:

- ◆ drawing conclusions from paragraphs
- ◆ drawing conclusions from business forms
- ◆ understanding visual information

You will learn how workers in the retail sales industry use these reading skills and materials in their work.

# Working as a Salesperson

**Words to Know**

commissions

consumer

merchandise

profit

sales associates

sales check

suggestion selling

Have you recently bought clothes? Furniture? A home appliance? If you bought an item in a retail store, you probably dealt with a salesperson. A retail store, or *retailer*, is a business that sells goods directly to customers. Retail salespeople are employees who help store customers with their purchases.

A salesperson listens to the customer's request. Then, he or she thinks about the merchandise in the store. Finally, the salesperson draws a conclusion about what merchandise would be best for the customer.

**Drawing conclusions** based on facts and information is an important sales skill. It also is an important reading skill. In this lesson, you will learn how to use the skill of drawing conclusions.

## Job Focus

**Salespeople** must be courteous, well groomed, and patient. They must know a lot about the items they are selling. They should have good math skills, since they work with prices. Most important, salespeople need good language skills. They should be good listeners. They must be able to find out what the customer wants. Good salespeople also give information and offer suggestions. They try to help customers make buying decisions.

Price charts, labels, product information, and magazine articles are some of the items that salespeople read. They also read letters, memos, and training materials.

There are more than 4 million jobs in retail sales. These jobs are expected to grow faster than the economy through the year 2005.

# Drawing Conclusions: How It Works

Drawing conclusions means forming a judgment based on information. To draw conclusions, you use information that you read to make a decision or form an opinion. You also use your own knowledge and experiences to draw conclusions.

To draw conclusions, ask yourself questions: "What are the main ideas? Are the facts reliable? Do things make sense? The answers will help you to make your own judgments about what you read.

Read the memo below.

---

**M e m o**

TO: **Sales associates**
FROM: Store manager
SUBJECT: Suggestion selling

Let's not forget the value of **suggestion selling.** This method is a good way to increase sales. Don't just ask, "Will that be all?" Suggest a specific item. To a customer buying a skateboard, suggest safety gear. To a customer buying a flashlight, recommend extra bulbs and batteries.

Suggestion selling makes the most of your time. You have already sold an item. With just a little more effort, you can add to the total **profit.**

Remember to make your suggestion after the customer has decided to buy but before you have written up the **sales check.**

---

**sales associates**
(saylz uh-SOH-shee-ayts)
salespeople who know store products and how to sell to customers

**suggestion selling**
(sug-JEHST-chun SEHL-ihng)
the method of recommending additional items to a customer who has made the decision to buy something

**profit** (PRAHF-iht) money left from a sale after expenses have been taken out

**sales check** (SAYLZ chehck) a store order form that lists items purchased

The main idea of the first paragraph is that suggestion selling is a good way to increase sales. Why is the store manager making this point? What conclusion can you draw?

*You can draw the conclusion that the store manager would like the sales staff to use suggestion selling.*

You can draw conclusions about each paragraph and about the entire memo. After thinking about the facts, opinions, and suggestions in the memo, what conclusions can you draw?

---

You might conclude *the store manager feels that the sales associates have not been using suggestion selling. The manager is reminding them to use this method to increase sales.*

The following article is from a magazine for salespeople. Read the article.

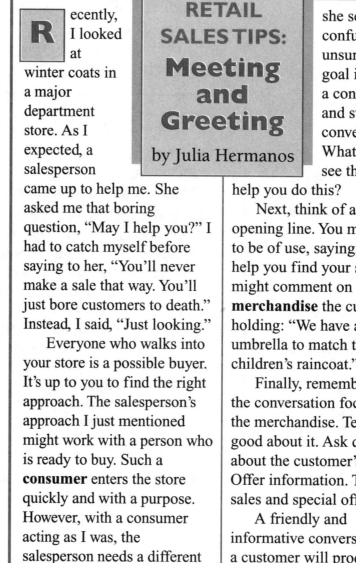

## RETAIL SALES TIPS:
# Meeting and Greeting
### by Julia Hermanos

Recently, I looked at winter coats in a major department store. As I expected, a salesperson came up to help me. She asked me that boring question, "May I help you?" I had to catch myself before saying to her, "You'll never make a sale that way. You'll just bore customers to death." Instead, I said, "Just looking."

Everyone who walks into your store is a possible buyer. It's up to you to find the right approach. The salesperson's approach I just mentioned might work with a person who is ready to buy. Such a **consumer** enters the store quickly and with a purpose. However, with a consumer acting as I was, the salesperson needs a different approach.

First, observe your customer. What products is she examining? Does she seem confused or unsure? Your goal is to make a connection and start a conversation. What do you see that can help you do this?

Next, think of a good opening line. You might offer to be of use, saying, "Can I help you find your size?" You might comment on **merchandise** the customer is holding: "We have an umbrella to match that children's raincoat."

Finally, remember to keep the conversation focused on the merchandise. Tell what is good about it. Ask questions about the customer's needs. Offer information. Talk about sales and special offers.

A friendly and informative conversation with a customer will produce good results. You'll make more sales, and you will create satisfied customers who come back for more.

Retail Sales                                                    19

**merchandise**
(MER-chun-dys) items for sale

**consumer** (kahn-SOOM-er) a person who buys goods and services

# CHECK YOUR UNDERSTANDING

Answer each question based on the selection on page 88.

1. What is *one* conclusion you can draw from the first paragraph?

    a. Salespeople are boring and not very helpful.

    b. Salespeople today rarely approach customers to make a sale.

    c. Asking "May I help you?" is not the best approach.

2. What conclusions can you draw from the second paragraph? (Choose *two.*)

    a. A salesperson needs to use the right approach for each customer.

    b. It may be easier to sell to a person who enters the store ready to buy.

    c. A good salesperson can sell a product to anyone who walks into the store.

3. What conclusions can you draw from the third paragraph? (Choose *two.*)

    a. A salesperson's goal is to observe the customers.

    b. Starting a conversation with a customer can help a salesperson make a sale.

    c. A salesperson can start a conversation by talking about a product the customer shows interest in.

In the last paragraph, the writer has drawn her own conclusions for the article. For each of the following conclusions about the whole article, underline **Agree** or **Disagree** to show how you feel about the writer's conclusion.

**Example: _Agree_ Disagree** Commenting on merchandise a customer is holding is a good opening line.

**Agree Disagree 4.** The question "May I help you?" is boring and not very effective for a salesperson to use.

**Agree Disagree 5.** A salesperson should think carefully about how to approach each customer and start a conversation.

**Agree Disagree 6.** A good conversation will often lead to a sale.

*Check your answers on page 120.*

James works as a salesperson in a men's clothing store. He has worked in the store for four years, and he has a number of steady customers. The customers are men who like James's sense of style and feel he helps them look good.

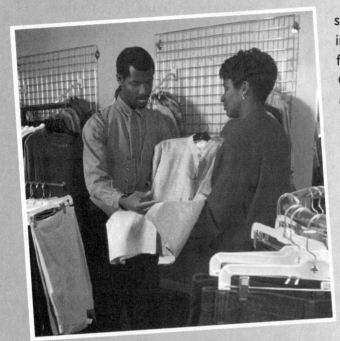

When a customer enters the store, James politely asks if he is interested in suits. James is good at figuring out a customer's tastes. Customers respect James's comments on the fit of a suit. James makes sure to take exact measurements for the tailor to follow.

When the customer has chosen a suit, James suggests a matching shirt and tie. James often increases the amount of the sale in this way. Finally, James writes up the sales check, accepts payment, and wraps up the purchases.

James has to do a lot of reading for his job. He reads labels, care instructions, price lists, and reports. He also reads men's magazines and fashion industry publications to keep up with men's styles.

James enjoys his job. He likes meeting new people and helping them choose clothing. Most of all, he enjoys working in a small store where he can make a difference in the store's profits.

The store manager wants to promote James to assistant manager. Then, James could help decide which merchandise to put in the store. James is planning to take some marketing courses to prepare for the promotion.

## TALK ABOUT IT

1. Discuss how James uses suggestion selling when a customer buys a suit.

2. What kinds of materials does James read for work?

3. Tell why James likes working in a small store.

**S**ales training is sometimes available for salespeople. Look at the information shown here.

# COMPUTER KING TRAINING PROGRAM

The Computer King Training Program was started in 1992. Over the years, we have revised and improved the program. All new salespeople are required to attend.

Our salespeople have praised the program. They say it helps them increase their sales and, of course, their **commissions.** Our statistics agree. We find that training improves the quality of the staff and the image of the store.

The program runs every day for two weeks. Employees attend classes and workshops. There is a handbook with written exercises. There are role-playing situations, where employees have the chance to try out skills. During breaks, employees get to know one another and share ideas.

Employees receive training in four key areas—selling skills, consumer information, product information, and industry knowledge.

Selling skills are a salesperson's best asset. They include listening to customers, presenting choices, handling customer objections, and closing a sale. Workshop leaders give many tips and exercises. Employees have a chance to practice.

Consumer information covers two areas. First, salespeople need to know what features and prices our customers request. Second, salespeople must know about consumer laws that affect us.

In product information, you will learn about our computers and their accessories. Experts will show how different products work. You will learn the advantages and disadvantages of different models. We will continue to hold product information sessions during the year for all salespeople. We want you to be able to answer every question your customer has.

The final area is industry knowledge. To be effective, you must keep up with changes in the industry. You must also know as much as possible about other stores that sell computers. They're our competitors. Our aim is to know what they are doing.

Training Program                                               ■ 3

Answer each question based on the selection on page 91.

1. What conclusion can you draw from the first paragraph?

   a. All stores have training programs.
   b. People promoted to salesperson from within the company need not attend the training program.
   c. Training is important at Computer King.

2. What conclusions can you draw from the second paragraph? (Choose *two*.)

   a. Computer King managers are concerned about staff quality.
   b. The training program has proven its value.
   c. Every store should have a sales training program.

3. What conclusions can you draw from the third paragraph? (Choose *two*.)

   a. Employees are expected to learn on their own.
   b. Reading and writing skills are needed in the program.
   c. The training presents practical, hands-on learning.

Write one reasonable conclusion that you can draw from each of the paragraphs named below. Use complete sentences.

**Example:** From the fifth paragraph, I draw the conclusion that *a salesperson needs great selling skills to be successful on the job.*

4. From the seventh paragraph, I draw the conclusion that

5. From the eighth paragraph, I draw the conclusion that

*Check your answers on page 120.*

## ◆ LESSON WRAP-UP

When you draw conclusions from writing, you are forming judgments about what you have read. Asking questions helps you to understand readings so that you can make judgments. Sometimes, drawing conclusions means forming an opinion or making a decision.

**1.** Imagine yourself in the following situations. What conclusions could you draw about how to act?

**Write a conclusion that you might draw for each situation.**

> a. Your supervisor is pleased with your work. She says that if you had more classes in accounting, you would qualify for a promotion.

I would conclude:

> b. Before going to work, you must take your child to a day-care center across town. Sometimes, the traffic is so bad that you are late for work. Your supervisor has mentioned that lateness is cause for firing.

I would consider:

**2.** Think of a situation in which someone tried to talk you into making a certain decision. For example, a caller might have tried to sell you something over the phone. A friend might have asked you to leave work early and go to a ballgame. How would you use the skill of drawing conclusions to come to a decision?

**Use your own words to describe the situation in the space below. Then finish the sentence that follows.**
Situation:

I would use the skill of drawing conclusions to:

*Check your answers on page 121.*

# Working as a Salesclerk

In many stores, the customers know what they want. They need only a little help. In these stores, salesclerks do much of the selling.

A salesclerk may stay behind a counter and accept payment for goods. He or she may answer questions. For example, a customer might ask, "Where can I find light bulbs?" or "Do you have ink refills for this kind of printer?"

Music stores, bookstores, grocery stores, toy stores, and hardware stores may have more salesclerks than salespeople. These stores often sell everyday items that are not expensive.

Salesclerks and other sales workers handle forms on the job. Reading forms and **drawing conclusions** from them is an important skill.

## Job Focus

**Salesclerks** deal with the public all day. They must be polite. Since they give information, they should have good language skills. More and more, salesclerks need to have computer skills.

Often, salesclerks work the cash register. They should be good with numbers. They must be able to focus on their work to avoid mistakes with money.

Salesclerks need to read sales slips, product information, and stock reports. They also receive office memos, letters, and other business papers.

Working as a salesclerk is a good way to begin a career in retail sales. A salesclerk has the chance to learn about sales and marketing. With experience, hard work, and additional education, a salesclerk can move up to salesperson or assistant manager.

# Drawing Conclusions: How It Works

Much of the information that we read on the job appears on different types of forms. It is important for workers to be able to read and understand forms. Salesclerks must often **draw conclusions** from forms. When you draw conclusions, you combine the information you read with what you already know to make decisions.

Read the cash-register receipt (ree-SEET).

**COLISEUM STATIONERS**

2174 Roosevelt Street, NY, NY 10017 212-555-9023

Register 2 Clerk 14 2:31 p.m. 06/20/——

| | |
|---|---|
| I CELLOPHANE TAPE | .99 |
| SUBTOTAL | .99 |
| TAX @ 8.25% | .08 |
| TOTAL | 1.07 |
| CASH PAYMENT | 1.10 |
| CASH CHANGE | .03 |

**Refund** within 7 days with cash-register receipt.

**refund** (REE-fund) a return of money to a customer in exchange for a return of merchandise to the store

The customer went to Coliseum Stationers on June 21 with this receipt to return a bottle of glue. What information would the salesclerk need to accept a return?

_____

*The salesclerk would need to know whether the glue was purchased at his or her store within the last seven days.* The salesclerk could find the name of the store and the date of purchase at the top of the receipt.

Did you notice that the receipt is for a purchase of cellophane tape? Yet, the customer wants to return a bottle of glue. What conclusion might the salesclerk draw?

_____

*The customer has probably brought the wrong receipt.* What decision should the salesclerk make about the return?

_____

*The salesclerk cannot take back the item and refund the money without the proper receipt.*

**R**ead the sales receipt to gather information about the customer's purchase.

## Melville Electronics

**Sales Check**   No. 1-5560
4121 Madison Street
Oakland, CA 94618
Phone 510-555-7879
Fax 510-555-7732

Wed., 5/23
Delivery date

Sold to   _Randy Mitchell_
Address   _627 Eliot Drive, Apt. 7B_
Phone   _570-555-1788_

| Date | Sold By | Check | Credit Card Type & Number |
|------|---------|-------|---------------------------|
| 5/21 | MLR | | Amex 0000-0630-000-99999 |

| Qty. | Item | Price | Amount |
|------|------|-------|--------|
| 1 | Hi-Tech TV Set, #622 | 229.99 | 229.99 |
| | | | |
| | | | |
| | | | |
| | | | |
| | | | |

**Service Contract:**
Declined

| | |
|---|---|
| Subtotal | 229.99 |
| Tax | 13.80 |
| Delivery | 8.00 |
| Total | 251.79 |

Special Instructions:
Use service elevator.

**service contract**
(SER-vihs KAHN-trakt) an agreement to pay a sum of money in exchange for repairs to equipment over a period of time

## CHECK YOUR UNDERSTANDING

Answer each question based on the sales receipt above.

1. How many items did the customer purchase?
   a. 622
   b. 3
   c. 1

2. How did the customer pay for the item?
   a. cash
   b. credit card
   c. check

**3.** What *day* of the week was the item purchased?

  a. Monday
  b. Wednesday
  c. Friday

**4.** Why do you think the owner of Melville Electronics wants to know who sold the merchandise?

**5.** What did the customer decide about a service contract?

**6.** Do customers have to pay tax on the delivery charge? How can you tell?

*Check your answers on page 121.*

## ON THE JOB

Elaine works as a salesclerk in a five-and-dime store. The store sells a wide variety of low-priced items. Household items like pots and dishes are sold there. Stationery, plants, yarn, clothes, and candy also are sold in the store.

Often, Elaine works the cash register. She rings up sales, takes payments, and bags purchases. She often has to read the store's weekly sales flyer to find the correct prices.

When sales are slow, Elaine's supervisor has her help on the sales floor. Elaine makes sure that items are in their proper place on the shelves. She moves displays and changes price signs. She also answers customers' questions and helps them find different items.

### TALK ABOUT IT

**1.** Think about the type of reading Elaine does on the job. Describe what kind of reading skills she might use.

**2.** Discuss what other kinds of skills Elaine uses on the job.

**DRAWING CONCLUSIONS**

**R**ead the store refund slip.

**refund slip** (REE-fund slihp) a written record of money returned to the customer in exchange for merchandise returned to the store

| REFUND SLIP | |
|---|---|
| **House Perfect** | Date __2/15__ |
| | Store no. __3__ |

| Customer's name | Phone |
|---|---|
| Andrea Chang | 319-555-6073 |

**Address** 26 Clarinda Lane  Cedar Rapids, IA 52321

| Item Returned | Amount | |
|---|---|---|
| 1 Melody tablecloth, yellow | 12 | 00 |
| 8 Melody napkins, yellow | 16 | 00 |
| Date of Purchase __2/13__   Tax | 1 | 12 |
| Total | 29 | 12 |

| Customer's signature | Employee 7 |
|---|---|
| *Andrea Chang* | **Authorization**  LR |

| Returned for | Reason for return |
|---|---|
| [ ] store credit | Too small for table. |
| [✓] cash refund | |
| [ ] credit card refund | |

CASH-REGISTER RECEIPT MUST BE STAPLED TO THIS SLIP.

**authorization** (aw-ther-eyez-AY-shun) approval for an action or transaction

## CHECK YOUR UNDERSTANDING

Answer each question based on the refund slip.

1. How long did the customer wait to return the merchandise?

    a. one day
    b. one week
    c. two days

2. How much will the store refund be?
    a. $12.00
    b. $29.12
    c. $28.00

3. How do you think the customer paid for the purchase?
    a. store charge
    b. cash
    c. credit card

4. What can you tell about the refund policy and cash register receipts?

**5.** Can an employee decide to make a refund on his or her own?

Circle **True** if a statement is true or **False** if a statement is false.

**True  False  6.** The store manager thinks that the customer has a good reason to return the merchandise.

**True  False  7.** There are three or more House Perfect stores.

**True  False  8.** The customer had to prove that she did not use the merchandise before the clerk would take it back.

*Check your answers on page 121.*

## ◆ LESSON WRAP-UP

Many forms are used on the job. They hold a lot of information. It is important to be able to read and draw conclusions from forms. Every item of information on a form has a purpose. To understand the purpose of an item, ask yourself, "Why is this item here?" The answer will help you understand how the information can be used.

Each of the following statements mentions a kind of form. What conclusions could you draw from reading the form?

Complete each statement.

**1.** By reading a medical form of a patient's first visit to a doctor's office, I could conclude

**2.** By reading a person's application for citizenship form, I could conclude

*Check your answers on page 121.*

# Working as a Stock Clerk

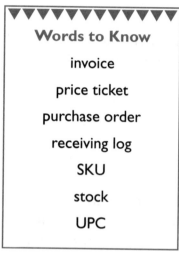

**Words to Know**

invoice

price ticket

purchase order

receiving log

SKU

stock

UPC

Receiving, storing, and counting goods are a major part of the retail sales business. First, store managers keep track of how many items they have to sell. They take an inventory, or count, of the items on the shelves.

Then, managers order the goods that they need. When the goods arrive, they must be checked. Then, the goods must be priced and put on the shelves for customers.

The goods that a store sells are the store's *stock*. Employees who unload, check, price, store, and arrange the stock are called *stock clerks*. To do their job, stock clerks get information from different sources. **Understanding visual information**—charts, diagrams, graphs, and other visuals—is an important reading skill in their work.

## Job Focus

**Stock clerks** can do many different tasks. In a large store, a stock clerk may be an expert at one task. For example, a clerk's main job might be putting prices on items. In a small store, the stock clerk may do many different tasks.

A stock clerk usually works in the part of the store where goods are received. This may be a stockroom or a warehouse. The clerk may open boxes, then check to see if any items are damaged or missing. In addition, some clerks may help with inventory. Inventory is a very important part of a business.

Stock clerks should be good at reading forms, labels, and numbers. They should be able to count quickly and correctly. They should feel comfortable with physical work and messy areas.

# Understanding Visual Information: How It Works

Workers often read information given in a graphic (GRAF-ihk), or a picture-like, form. The form may be a drawing, chart, diagram, or graph. Words, numbers, and symbols are included to help make the meaning clear.

Different types of graphics are good for showing different things. Tables, graphs, and charts are good for showing information about numbers. Maps, floor plans, and seating plans are good for showing how items are arranged in a space. Diagrams, flowcharts, and timelines are useful for showing steps in a process.

Read the graph shown here.

**stock** (stahk) merchandise on hand to be sold

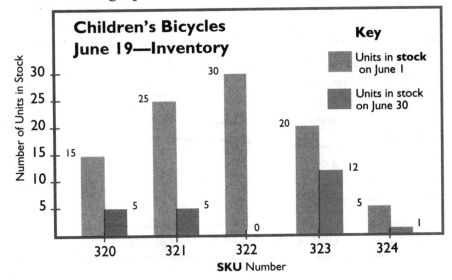

**SKU** a code number that a store gives to a product (SKU stands for stock-keeping unit)

What information does the title tell you?

_The title tells you that this graph is based on the June inventory of children's bicycle._ Reading the title gives you a preview of the graph.

Next, read any labels, keys, or instructions. Make sure to read all the writing that explains the graph. What does the key tell you about the bar graph?

_The key tells you which bar stands for stock on June 1 and which stands for stock on June 30._ You could not understand the graph without this information.

Now you can use informaton to answer questions. For example, what was the most popular bicycle?

*SKU 322 was the most popular. There were 30 in stock on June 1. None remained in stock by June 30.*

**R**eview the chart below.

invoice (IHN-voys) a bill from a supplier listing the goods sent or sold

purchase order (PER-chus AW-der) a written request from a buyer to a supplier for goods

receiving log (rih-SEEV-ihng lahg) a written record of goods received

UPC a product label made up of lines and numbers that can be read electronically (UPC is short for universal product code)

price ticket a tag on an item that gives the price as well as other information

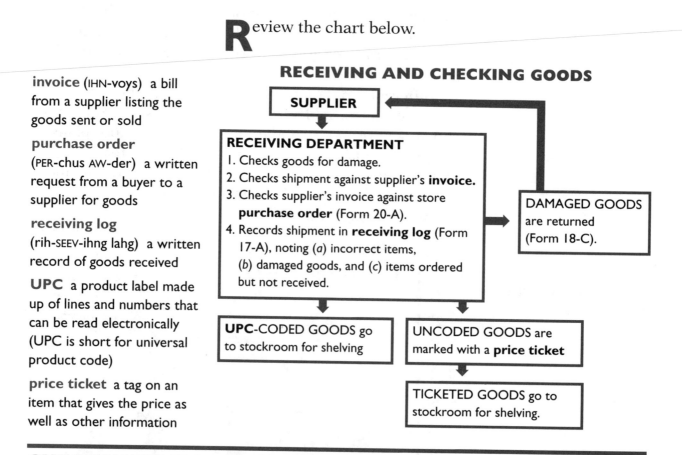

## RECEIVING AND CHECKING GOODS

**SUPPLIER**

**RECEIVING DEPARTMENT**
1. Checks goods for damage.
2. Checks shipment against supplier's **invoice.**
3. Checks supplier's invoice against store **purchase order** (Form 20-A).
4. Records shipment in **receiving log** (Form 17-A), noting (*a*) incorrect items, (*b*) damaged goods, and (*c*) items ordered but not received.

**DAMAGED GOODS** are returned (Form 18-C).

**UPC**-CODED GOODS go to stockroom for shelving

**UNCODED GOODS** are marked with a **price ticket**

**TICKETED GOODS** go to stockroom for shelving.

## CHECK YOUR UNDERSTANDING

Answer each question based on the chart above.

**1.** What role does the supplier have in this chart?
   a. The supplier makes the goods.
   b. The supplier ships the goods.
   c. The supplier shelves the goods.

**2.** What document does the store receive with the shipment from the supplier?
   a. purchase order
   b. invoice
   c. receiving log

**3.** What document must the receiving department fill out?
   a. purchase order
   b. invoice
   c. receiving log

Circle **True** if is a statement is true or **False** if a statement is false.

**True   False**   **4.** The chart tells who writes up the purchase order.

**True   False**   **5.** After the shipment is checked, the undamaged goods are divided into two groups: those with UPC codes and those without codes.

**True   False**   **6.** The supplier's invoice lists the items in the shipment.

**7.** Does this chart describe a process (how things should happen) or a place? Explain.

*Check your answers on page 121.*

## ON THE JOB

Manny felt lucky to get his job as a stock clerk at Jack's Sporting Goods. Manny is a sports fan, and he often bought items at Jack's. As an employee, he gets a 20 percent discount on items as well as good training in retail sales.

Jack hired him because Manny is prompt, dependable, and eager to learn. Manny's job is to unload shipments, open boxes, and stock shelves. He is learning how to check the shipments and price the goods. Manny also keeps the store swept and clean.

On the job, Manny reads labels, shipping invoices, purchase orders, and other forms. He fills out stock and inventory reports. He hopes one day to become a sporting goods salesperson for a large retail store.

### TALK ABOUT IT

**1.** Explain why reading is important in Manny's job.

**2.** Describe how Manny's interest in sports might help him do his job better.

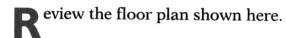

Review the floor plan shown here.

## SHOE CITY STOCKROOM FLOOR PLAN

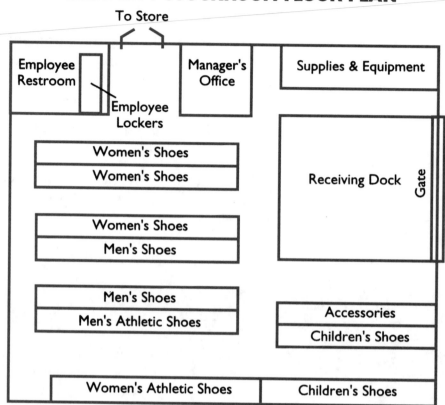

---

## CHECK YOUR UNDERSTANDING

Answer each question based on the floor plan above.

1. Where is the manager's office?

   a. near the entrance to the store
   b. near the children's shoes
   c. on another floor

2. What merchandise has the most shelf space?

   a. men's shoes
   b. women's shoes
   c. children's shoes

3. Why do you think the women's shoes are closest to the store entrance?

   a. Most of the shoes in stock are women's shoes.
   b. Most of the salespeople are women.
   c. Most of the customers are women.

**LESSON 14 ◆ WORKING AS A STOCK CLERK**

**4.** Why do you think the equipment is near the receiving dock?



**5.** If you entered from the store and wanted to go to the children's shoes section, what direction would you walk?



**6.** If you were the manager, how would you organize shoes within each group: by color? by manufacturer? by size? Explain your choice.

I would organize shoes by


Explanation:



*Check your answers on page 121.*


## ◆ LESSON WRAP-UP

Information appears in graphic form as well as in paragraphs. Some graphics are tables, charts, graphs, diagrams, floor plans, and maps.

Following a step-by-step process can help you read graphics. Always read the title first. Next, read any labels, keys, or other writing that explains items in a graphic. Apply reading skills you have learned, like comparing and contrasting or drawing conclusions. Finally, read the whole graphic.

Graphics are in newspapers, magazines, and on TV. They are used on the job. And they are used in stores on product labels. Think of a graphic you have seen. What skills would you use to get information from it?

Select a graphic. Then, finish the sentence that follows.

Graphic:
To get information from this graphic, I would


*Check your answers on page 121.*

# ◆ UNIT FOUR REVIEW

1. Write a brief paragraph to explain why you might need to draw a conclusion on the job or about a person.

2. When you apply for a job, you must fill out forms. What information do you think is needed on these forms? What conclusions could someone draw from the information on the forms? Answer those questions in one or two sentences for each of the following forms.

   a. Job application form:

   b. Tax form:

3. Choose a graphic that would be used to give information for the following items. Write one to two sentences to explain why you chose that graphic.

   a. To show where products are located in a retail store:

   b. To show how a purchase order form goes from the store office to the supplier:

   c. To show how a delivery truck gets from the store to a customer's home:

*Check your answers on page 122.*

# RESPELLING GUIDE

Use the following guide to help you pronounce long
and hard words.

| Sound | Respelling | Example of Respelling |
|---|---|---|
| **a** as in hat | a | hat |
| **a** as in day, date, paid | ay | day, dayt, payd |
| **vowels** as in far, on, bother, hot | ah | fahr, ahn, BAH-thuhr, haht |
| **vowels** as in dare, air, heir | ai | dair, air, air |
| **vowels** as in saw, call, pore, door | aw | saw, kawl, pawr, dawr |
| **e** as in pet, debt | eh | peht, deht |
| **e** as in seat, beef, chief, **y** as in beauty | ee | seet, beef, cheef BYOO-tee |
| **vowels** as in learn, urn, fur, sir | er | lern, ern, fer, ser |
| **i** as in sit, bitter, **ee** as in been | ih | siht, BIHT-uhr, bihn |
| **i** as in mile, **ei** as in height | eye | meyel, heyet |
| **o** as in go | oh | goh |
| **vowels** as in boil, toy | oi | boil, toi |
| **vowels** as in how, out, bough | ow | how, owt, bow |
| **vowels** as in up, come | u | up, kum |
| **vowels** as in use, use, bureau, few | yoo | yooz yoose, BYOO-roh, fyoo |
| **vowels** as in look, put, foot | oo | look, poot, foot |
| **vowels** as in bitter, act**io**n | uh | BIHT-uhr, AK-shuhn |

Consonants are respelled as they sound. Here are a
few examples.

| | | |
|---|---|---|
| **c** as in cat | k | kat |
| **c** as in dance | s | dans |
| **ch** as in Christmas | k | KRIHS-muhs |
| **g** as in gem | j | jehm |
| **s** as in laser | z | LAY-zuhr |
| **ph** as in phone | f | fohn |

# RESOURCES

*The following organizations and publications may provide more information about the jobs covered in this book.*

**United States Government**
**U.S. Department of Labor, Employment and Training Administration**

Adult Training Programs include the following:
Job Training Partnership Act (JTPA)
This program provides job training for disadvantaged adults who face significant employment barriers. For more information, write:

Office of Employment and Training
Programs, Room N4469
U.S. Department of Labor
200 Constitution Ave, N.W.
Washington, DC 20210
ON THE INTERNET: http://www.doleta.gov/
programs/programs.htm

Apprenticeship Training
The Bureau of Apprenticeship and Training registers apprenticeship programs in 23 states. It also assists State Apprenticeship Councils in 27 states, the District of Columbia, Puerto Rico, and the U.S. Virgin Islands. For further information, write or call:

Bureau of Apprenticeship and Training
U.S. Department of Labor
200 Constitution Ave, N.W.
Washington, DC 20210
(202) 219-5921
ON THE INTERNET: http://www.doleta.gov/
programs/programs.htm

The Bureau of Labor Statistics has descriptions of working conditions for a wide variety of specific occupational areas. For more information on the Bureau's

publications, write to:

Bureau of Labor Statistics
Division of Information Services
2 Massachusetts Avenue, N.E.
Room 2860
Washington, DC 20212
Information specialists provide a variety of services by telephone: (202)606-5886
To send a question by fax, please call
(202) 606-7890
ON THE INTERNET: http://stats.bls.gov

For general career information and a directory of accredited private career and technical schools offering programs in the job areas covered by this book, write to:

Accrediting Commission of
Career Schools
2101 Wilson Blvd.
Suite 302
Arlington, VA 22201

## Unit 1 TRAVEL AND RECREATION JOBS

American Society of Travel Agents
Education Department
1101 King Street
Alexandria, VA 22314
ON THE INTERNET: http://www.astanet.com

The Institute of Certified Travel Agents
148 Linden Street
P. O. Box 812059
Wellesley, MA 02181-0012
(800) 542-4282

Reference books:
"Your Career in Travel & Tourism," Merton House Publishing Company, 937 West Liberty Drive, Wheaton, IL 60187.
"The Travel Agent"—Dealer in Dreams,"

Kendal/Hunt Publishing Company, Dubuque, IA 52004

"Flying High in Travel: A Complete Guide to Careers in the Travel Industry," Karen Rubin, John Wiley & Sons, Inc.

American Automobile Association
http://www.aaa.com/welcome.html

## Unit 2 JOBS WORKING WITH CHILDREN

National Association for Sport & Physical Education
1900 Association Drive
Reston, VA 20191
PHONE: (800) 213-7193
FAX: (703) 476-8316

American Camping Association, Inc.
5000 State Road 67 North
Martinsville, IN 46151-7902
PHONE: (317) 342-8456
FAX: (317) 342-2065

## Unit 3 HOTEL AND RESTAURANT JOBS

American Hotel and Motel Association (AHMA)
1201 New York Avenue, NW
Washington, DC 20005-3931
PHONE: (202) 289-3100
FAX (202) 289-3199
ON THE INTERNET: http://www.ahma.com
Lodging Magazine, published by the AHMA

Educational Institute of the American Hotel and Motel Association (AHMA)
1407 S. Harrison Rd., Ste. 300
East Lansing, MI 48823
PHONE: (517) 353-5500
FAX: (517) 353-5527
TOLL-FREE: 1-800-752-4567
ON THE INTERNET: info@ei-ahma.org

Ask about Instructional Resources/Hospitality Curricula for use at high school and post-secondary levels. Discover how Professional Certification can give you or your employees industry-wide recognition for hospitality expertise.

Council on Hotel, Restaurant, and Institutional Education
1200 17th Street NW
Washington, DC 20036-3097
ON THE INTERNET: http://www.access.digex. net/~alliance/

National Restaurant Association
1200 Seventeenth Street, N.W.
Washington, DC 20036-3097
PHONE: (202) 331-5900
ON THE INTERNET: http://www.restaurant.org/

About The Educational Foundation of the National Restaurant Association
250 South Wacker Drive
Suite 1400
Chicago, IL 60606
A not-for-profit organization based in Chicago, The Educational Foundation is the primary source of education, training, and professional development for the foodservice industry.
ON THE INTERNET: http://www.restaurant.org/ educate/about.htm

United Food and Commercial Workers Union
1775 K Street NW
Washington, DC 20006-1502

## Unit 4 RETAIL SALES JOBS

National Retail Federation
325 Seventh Street NW
Suite 1000
Washington, DC 20004-2802
(202) 783-7971
ON THE INTERNET: http://www.nrf.com

# GLOSSARY

**amount tendered** money given as payment

**annual** yearly; every year

**applicant** a person who asks for a job

**auditorium** a large room with many seats

**authorization** approval for an action or transaction

**balancing the cash** accounting for the day's sales and money; also called balancing the till

**balcony** an upper level of a theater that extends from the back wall part way over the lower level

**brochures** small booklets of information

**campers** people going to camp

**cash register** a machine that records sales, stores cash from sales, and gives receipts

**chauffeur** a person licensed to drive a car or limousine for hire

**chauffeurs' license** a state-issued license to drive a commercial vehicle such as a bus

**child abuse** cruel or physically harmful acts against children; child abuse is a crime

**clients** customers

**commissions** fee paid given to salespeople for a completed sale; usually a percentage of the amount of the sale

**complimentary** free of charge

**conference** a meeting between two or more people to talk about a specific subject

**consumer** a person who buys goods and services

**continental breakfast** a light morning snack

**convention** a general meeting of members of a group

**counselor** a person who supervises people at a camp

**day camp** a place where children go for sports and play during the day in the summer

**Department of Health** a city or state government office that protects people's health

**depot** a place where buses or trains begin their route; also called a terminal or station

**discount** a reduction in price

**discriminate** to refuse to serve a customer for reasons such as the customer's race, religion, sex, or ethnic background

**double occupancy** rental of a hotel room by two people

**employee** a person who is hired to work for wages or salary

**evaluation report** a written form that gives facts and opinions about a person or situation

**even** the same amount of cash in the drawer as recorded on the cash-register tape

**family day care** a small business in which a person provides care for children in the provider's home

**first aid** steps for caring for cuts, scrapes, and other injuries

**flier** a printed sheet of paper, usually folded, which contains information

**garnishes** food used as decoration, like parsley or a slice of fruit

**gratis** free of charge

**hack license** a driving permit to drive a taxi or car for hire; also known as a taxi driver's license

**Heimlich maneuver** an emergency technique to help choking victims

**hygiene** conditions, such as cleanliness, that are good for health

**ingredients** things combined together to make a food

**inventory** a count of items on hand to be sold

**invoice** a bill from a supplier listing the goods sent or sold

**memo** a written message sent within a company

**menu** a list of foods that may be ordered in a restaurant

**merchandise** items for sale

**odometer** an instrument in a car that records mileage

**orchestra level** the main floor of a theater

**over** more cash than the amount recorded on the cash-register tape

**paraprofessional** a specially trained person who works with teachers, lawyers, or other professionals

**price ticket** a tag on an item that gives the price as well as other information

**professional** skilled; highly trained

**profit** money left from a sale after expenses have been taken out

**purchase order** a written request from a buyer to a supplier for goods

**radio fare** a passenger assigned by the radio dispatcher

**receiving log** a written record of goods received

**refund** a return of money to a customer in exchange for a return of merchandise to the store

**refund slip** a written record of money returned to the customer in exchange for merchandise returned to the store

**registration** an official listing or record

**reservation** a promise to hold a space

**route** a planned path or course of travel

**sales associate** salespeople in a retail store who know store products and how to sell to customers

**sales check** a store order form that lists items purchased

**service contract** an agreement to pay a sum of money in exchange for repairs to equipment over a period of time

**setup** preparation of a dining room for business

**short** less cash than the amount recorded on the cash-register tape

**single occupancy** rental of a hotel room by one person

**SKU** short for stockkeeping unit; a code number that a store gives to a product

**stock** merchandise on hand to be sold

**suggestion selling** the method of recommending additional items to a customer who has made the decision to buy something

**suites** hotel unit with more than one room (in addition to the bathroom)

**superintendent** a supervisor of a school system

**supervise** to watch over or control

**taximeter** an instrument in a taxicab that measures distance traveled and computes fares

**teacher's aide** a person who works in a classroom helping the teacher

**terrace** patio

**timetable** listings of departure and arrival times for buses, trains, airplanes, or boats; also called schedules

**tourist** someone who is traveling, often for sightseeing

**transactions** payments for a purchase

**trip record** a log showing the details of taxi rides during a shift

**UPC** short for universal product code; a product label made up of lines and numbers that can be read electronically

**utensils** items such as knives, forks, and spoons used for eating or cooking

**GLOSSARY**

# INDEX

## A
assistant coach, 50
assistant manager, 90, 94
assistant superintendent, 44

## B
bus driver, 1, 16, 20

## C
camp counselor, 46
camp director, 48
cashier, 55, 72, 74, 76
chauffeur, 9, 10
checker, 72, 73
chef, 56, 58
child-care provider, 32, 36
child-care worker, 31
classroom assistant, 31, 40, 42, 44
coach, 31, 46, 51
cook, 56, 61
counselor, 31, 46, 47, 48

## D
day-care worker, 32
director, 34, 51
dishwasher, 61
driver, 1, 16, 18, 19, 20

## F
food preparer, 56
food server, 78
food service worker, 78

## H
head cook, 58
hired car driver, 8
hotel clerk, 64, 68

## I
intercity bus driver, 16

## L
local transit bus driver, 16

## M
manager, 90
mechanic, 12, 13

## P
paraprofessional, 44
pie maker, 58
preschool teacher, 32

## R
referee, 50
retail salesperson, 86

## S
salad person, 61
sales associates, 87, 88
sales attendant, 151
salesclerk, 94, 95, 97
salesperson, 86, 90
school bus driver, 16
server, 78, 79, 81, 82
short-order cook, 56
stock clerk, 100, 103
store manager, 87, 90
superintendent, 44
supervisor, 97
supplier, 102

## T
tailor, 90
taxi driver, 8, 10, 11, 12
taxicab driver, 1
teacher, 31, 32, 40, 41, 43, 45
teacher's aide, 44
ticket seller, 24, 29
tourist guide, 2, 4

## W
waiter, 78
waitress, 78

# ANSWER KEY

## UNIT ONE: TRAVEL AND RECREATION JOBS

### Lesson 1: Guiding Tourists and Visitors

**CHECK YOUR UNDERSTANDING**

*page 4*

1. b
2. b
3. c
4. b

**CHECK YOUR UNDERSTANDING**

page 6

1. c
2. b
3. a
4. b
5. c

**LESSON WRAP UP**

*page 7*

Your answers may be similar to these:

1. No matter where you shop for groceries, prices keep going up.
2. A neighborhood watch is just one way to help prevent crime.
3. The nightly news is one of the most violent shows on television.

### Lesson 2: Driving a Taxicab or Car for Hire

**CHECK YOUR UNDERSTANDING**

*page 11*

Your answers may be something like these:

1. You must file an exam application in person. You can file on Mondays, Wednesdays, and Fridays from 9:00 A.M. to noon and on Tuesdays and Thursdays from 1:00 to 5:00 P.M. You must pay a $25.00 fee. You must bring certain documents when you apply.
2. When you go to take the exam, bring your admission card, a pen, your driver's license, and proof that you are legally able to work in the United States (birth certificate, passport, or other papers).
3. The main idea of paragraph 4 is that the exam, which has four written parts and one oral part, covers the basic skills and knowledge a taxi driver needs.
4. The bulleted points describe the different parts of the exam. They state the knowledge and skills needed on the job.

**CHECK YOUR UNDERSTANDING**

*page 14*

1. b
2. a
3. c
4. b
5. a
6. b
7. a

**LESSON WRAP UP**

*page 15*

Your answers may be something like these:

1. I would ask if the interviewer asked a lot of questions, if the interviewer seemed happy with the answers, and if salary and hours were discussed.
2. Main idea: It was a great concert. Details: The band played all its big hits and gave three encores.
3. Main idea: The movie was about family and love.
Details: The movie showed many scenes with different family members talking, and they talked a lot about their relationships with the people they love.

### Lesson 3: Driving Passengers on a Bus

**CHECK YOUR UNDERSTANDING**

*page 19*

1. a
2. c

3. b

4. Most bus stops will be along 2 streets: Michigan Avenue and Georgia Avenue.

5. Whitman Park is bordered by Nebraska Boulevard, Georgia Avenue, and 5th Street.

6. Yes

7. Yes

8. No

9. No

10. Yes

11. Yes

## CHECK YOUR UNDERSTANDING

*page 21*

1. a

2. c

3. c

4. c

5. c

6. Bus 1702 at 7:05

7. Bus 1709 at 9:32

8. Bus 1704 at 7:53

9. Bus 1708

10. Bus 1711

## LESSON WRAP UP

*page 23*

Your answers may be something like these:

1. a. You would infer that your niece needs to be vaccinated within the coming year.

   b. You would infer that there will not be any meat or fish served at dinner.

2. By reading between the lines, I see that Jean wants me to volunteer to help her move.


## Lesson 4: Selling Tickets

## CHECK YOUR UNDERSTANDING

*page 26*

1. b

2. a

3. c

4. K-202 to K-210

5. Seat K-105 faces the right of the stage.

6. F-301

7. BB-211 to BB-216

## CHECK YOUR UNDERSTANDING

*page 28*

1. True

2. True

3. False

4. False

5. False

6. False

7. 3 x $10 = $30 total weekend fee

8. 1 x $7.50 = $7.50; 2 x $3.75 = $7.50; $7.50 + $7.50 = $15.00 total weekday fee

9. 2 x $5.00 = $10.00; 1 x $10.00 = $10.00; $10.00 + $10.00 = $20.00 total weekend fee

## LESSON WRAP UP

*page 29*

Your answers may be something like these:

1. I can use the price chart at a movie theater to find many important details. Price charts usually list the cost of tickets for regular and matinee showings, as well as ticket costs for children and seniors. There are also price charts that show how much popcorn, drinks, and other snacks cost.

2. I would find a TV schedule helpful. I could locate the day, time, and channel for different shows and movies. It would save me time to look up the information instead of flipping through the channels and landing on TV ads.

## UNIT ONE REVIEW

*page 30*

Your answers may be something like these:

1. First, find the topic of the paragraph. The topic is a word or phrase that describes the general subject of the paragraph. Next, ask yourself, "What is the main point the writer wants to tell about this topic?" The major focus of the paragraph or point that the writer wants to make is the main idea.

2. A lot of people apply for the same job. Many jobs require experience and job skills. You have to search to find out about job openings.

3. Making inferences means using clues and hints to uncover information. For example, suppose a description tells when a company was started. You can use the date to infer how many years the company has been in business.

4. a. Chart: It can be used to organize price information.

b. Timetable: It can be used to organize bus and train schedule information.

c. Diagram: It can be used to organize information about seating in a concert hall.

## UNIT TWO: JOBS WORKING WITH CHILDREN

### Lesson 5: Providing Child-Care Services

**CHECK YOUR UNDERSTANDING**
*page 34*
1. b
2. c
3. a
4. b
5. c
6. b
7. b

Your answers may be similar to these:

8. Numbering the list of instructions would show that the steps follow a certain order. It would make it easier if you could refer to the step by number.

9. No, because the items to be packed are not steps, and they can be done in any order.

**CHECK YOUR UNDERSTANDING**
*page 38*
1. c
2. c
3. b
4. Call to make a registration appointment.
5. There are four forms: the Registration Application, the State Central Register form for a child abuse and maltreatment background check, the Medical Record form for the provider and other household members, and the Request for Fire Department Approval form.

6. Anita must attend an information and training workshop.

7. Registration entitles the provider to free training and assistance. Registration shows the parent that the provider's home is safe for children.

**LESSON WRAP UP**
*page 39*
Your answers may be similar to these:

1. It is easier to follow directions when I read through the directions before I start. It also helps if I gather all of the materials and tools I need before I start.

2. If I have trouble following directions, I could look at any pictures that come with the directions. I also could check the directions again. Finally, I could ask someone to read the directions as I do each step

### Lesson 6: Helping in the Classroom

**CHECK YOUR UNDERSTANDING**
*page 42*
1. True
2. False
3. False
4. True
5. Amelia should start helping the children dress at 2:20.
6. Amelia needs to know which children are in group A, which she must take to the library. Amelia also needs to know where the library is located.
7. D, B, A, C

**CHECK YOUR UNDERSTANDING**
*page 44*
1. Session A, Working with Difficult Children, and Session B, Safety in the Playground, are given at 9:40.
2. The 11:20 speech will take 40 minutes.
3. The conference will take 4 $\frac{1}{2}$ hours.
4. Superintendent Ruben Suarez is scheduled to speak at 9:00.
5. Session A at 9:40 might be helpful.
6. Session A at 10:40 might be useful.

## LESSON WRAP UP

*page 45*

Your answers may be something like these:

1. Get interview clothes ready.

   Eat something so I won't be hungry during the interview.

   Wash up and get ready to get dressed.

   Get dressed.

   Leave so I have enough time to catch the bus.

   Catch a bus that gets me to the interview at least 15 minutes early.

2. Get interview clothes ready.

   Pick out clothes that match.

   Make sure they are clean and wrinkle-free.

   Check shoes; polish them if needed.

## Lesson 7: Coaching and Counseling Children

### CHECK YOUR UNDERSTANDING

*page 49*

1. a. fact
   b. opinion
   c. opinion
2. a. fact
   b. opinion
   c. opinion
3. a. fact
   b. fact
   c. opinion
4. a. opinion
   b. fact
   c. opinion
5. a
6. b

### CHECK YOUR UNDERSTANDING

*page 52*

1. a
2. a
3. a
4. b

Your answers may be similar to these:

5. Basketball is the most exciting team sport to watch.

6. Learning to play as a team is not as much fun as taking all the shots yourself.

## LESSON WRAP UP

*page 53*

Your answers may be similar to these:

1. The United States gives citizens a chance to get a basic education. It is important for people to get a good education. A good education will help you get a better job.

2. I punch a time card each day when I start and stop my work.

   I get paid for overtime.

   The company gives health insurance to full-time employees.

## UNIT TWO REVIEW

*page 54*

1. Step 1: Preview the directions. Read the directions and look at any illustrations.
   Step 2: Prepare for the tasks. Assemble ingredients and materials. Make sure you have enough time.
   Step 3: Follow the directions. Read and do each step of the directions.
   Step 4: Review your work. Make sure everything worked well.

2. Step 1: Preview the schedule. For example, read through a list of appointments you might have.
   Step 2: Prepare your work. For example, assemble the items you need for each appointment.
   Step 3: Review the schedule. For example, look at your watch to make sure you are on time for your next appointment.

3. b. Fact: She smiles often and does not complain about her job.
   c. Opinion: The food is delicious.
   d. Fact: His players score the highest and use the hardest plays.
   e. Opinion: This is a popular camp for children.
   f. Fact: The teacher's aide told me that she loves working with children.

# UNIT THREE: HOTEL AND RESTAURANT JOBS

## Lesson 8: Preparing Food

### CHECK YOUR UNDERSTANDING
*page 59*

1. The column headings are Monday, Tuesday, Wednesday, Thursday, and Friday.

2. The row headings are sugar buns, cheese Danish, fruit Danish, bagels, blueberry pies, apple pies, and special.

3. The menu covers the week of May 20.

4. There are five fillings listed: cheese (for Danish), fruit (for Danish), apple, blueberry, and peach.

5. There are three kinds of frozen items: pie crusts, Danish pastry sheets, and sugar buns.

6. a

7. c

8. c

9. Carlos must order 13 pie crusts. He has two on hand and must make 15 pies for the week.

10. Carlos needs to order 1 can of blueberry pie filling. He has 1 1/2 cans on hand and must make 5 pies.

### CHECK YOUR UNDERSTANDING
*page 62*

1. Menu item, side dishes, garnish, salad, and bread are the column headings.

2. Hamburger, Hamburger Deluxe, Grilled Chicken Platter, Fried Fish Platter, and Vegetarian Chili are the categories shown in the row headings.

3. Pickle, cole slaw, lemon wedge, tartar sauce, grated cheddar cheese, and sour cream belong under the garnish heading.

4. The hamburger category contains no side dishes.

5. Three categories contain salad as a side dish.

6. Your answer may be something like this: Garnish the grilled chicken platter with 1/4 pickle and a lemon wedge.

7. Your answer may be something like this: Use 1/2 cup rice as a side dish for the vegetarian chili. Garnish the platter with 1 tablespoon grated cheddar and a sour cream cup. Serve it with a salad and a roll and butter.

8.

| MENU ITEM | SIDE DISHES | GARNISH | SALAD | BREAD |
|---|---|---|---|---|
| Roast Turkey Platter | 1/2 cup rice | Cranberry sauce cup | Yes | Roll & butter |

### LESSON WRAP-UP
*page 63*

Your answers may be something like these:

1. The information on the dog food bag is probably in table form because it makes it easier to use. Using the row and column headings, I can easily find how much food I should feed my dog. It depends on how much he weighs and whether I use dry dog food or dry and canned dog food mixed together.

2. For information about long-distance travel, I would look up numbers for some form of transportation: airlines, bus, train, or rental cars. I might also look for hotel 800 numbers to book a room in advance.

## Lesson 9: Taking Care of Guests

### CHECK YOUR UNDERSTANDING
*page 67*

1. b

2. c

3. c

4. Mr. Guest is traveling to Hope to attend a wedding.

5. Mr. Guest will stay at the hotel for two nights—Friday, June 4, and Saturday, June 5.

6. The single room costs more per person.

7. Rates for children over ten are higher.

8. False

9. True

10. True
## CHECK YOUR UNDERSTANDING
*page 69*
1. a
2. b
3. c
4. c
5. a. $40
  b. $80
  c. $35
  d. $70
  e. The total for two people in single rooms is $80. The total for two people in one double room is $70. The double room is less expensive.

## LESSON WRAP-UP
*page 71*
Your answers may be similar to these:
1. I compared two ads about apartments for rent. The rent for one apartment was $275, and the rent for the other apartment was $350. One apartment had 1 bath, while the other apartment had 1 1/2 baths. One apartment had a balcony, and the other one didn't.
2. Two more job characteristics could be "Working overtime" and "Working with computers."

## Lesson 10: Working at a Cash Register
### CHECK YOUR UNDERSTANDING
*page 74*
1. The customer will be less likely to argue later.
2. Use as few coins as possible.
3. The customer may get angry.
4. The customer is confused.
5. The customer is satisfied.
6. The customer can see the bill on the ledge.

### CHECK YOUR UNDERSTANDING
*page 76*
1. b
2. c

3. a
4. short
5. over
6. short
7. even
8. b

## LESSON WRAP-UP
*page 77*
Your answers may be something like these:
1. a. Cause: a traffic accident on the highway
  b. Effect: traffic was backed up for miles
2. a. Cause: heavy traffic on the highway
  b. Effect: many people were late for work
3. a. Cause: only two cashiers working
  b. Effect: long lines at the checkout counters

## Lesson 11: Serving Food
### CHECK YOUR UNDERSTANDING
*page 80*
1. since
2. because
3. so that
4. if
5. then
6. Placemats make cleanup easier.
7. All settings look the same.
8. The glasses will stay clean.

### CHECK YOUR UNDERSTANDING
*page 82*
1. if
2. as a result
3. so that
4. then
5. The machine will not work properly.
6. Clogging or overflow may occur.
7. The steamer does not become clogged.
8. There is less risk of damage and injury.
9. Your answer may be something like this: Because the new server filled the filter too full, the espresso machine overflowed.

10. Your answer may be something like this: Injury can happen if the equipment is used improperly.

**LESSON WRAP-UP**

*page 83*

Your answers may be something like these:

1. If you want a tax refund, you have to file your taxes.

2. Because I get sick from milk, I try to avoid anything made with milk.

3. As a result of working overtime, my paycheck was a lot bigger than usual.

**UNIT THREE REVIEW**

*page 84*

Your answers may be something like these:

1. The hotel clerk accepts payments from guests. The food server may or may not accept payment from customers. The hotel clerk waits for guest to approach. The food server moves around from customer to customer all day. Both hotel clerk and food server must be pleasant and even-tempered with the people they serve.

2. The pros about being a cashier are that it's not hard physical work, you can work in a place where there is a lot of activity, and you are trusted with money.

The cons about being a cashier are that you must sometimes deal with difficult customers, it is easy to make mistakes with money, and you do the same thing over and over again.

3. a. Did the machine break down? Did a worker do something wrong?

b. Were the prices too high? What did customers think of the food?

4. a. Did the guest complain to the manager? Did the manager talk to the hotel clerk about the event?

b. Did the cashier make mistakes? Did the manager warn the cashier about the problem?

5. a. I applied for a job in a day-care center because I like working with children.

b. If I can get a job as a hotel clerk, I will work hard for a promotion.

c. She memorized the menu so that she could write up food orders quickly.

# UNIT FOUR: RETAIL SALES JOBS

## Lesson 12: Working as a Salesperson

**CHECK YOUR UNDERSTANDING**

*page 89*

1. c
2. a, b
3. b, c

Your reasons for choosing agree or disagree may be something like these:

4. Agree: The writer shows that customers usually respond by saying, "Just looking." Disagree: I often like it when a salesperson asks, "May I help you?" Then it is up to me to get help or not.

5. Agree: The author shows that thinking about your approach can lead to a successful conversation. Disagree: I think experienced salespeople just know what to do.

6. Agree: It makes sense to me that people are more likely to buy when the salesperson talks nicely. Disagree: The writer has not really shown how the conversation leads to a sale. It seems as though the customer could just end the conversation and leave.

**CHECK YOUR UNDERSTANDING**

*page 92*

1. c
2. a, b
3. b, c

Your answers may be something like these:

4. Computer King wants to provide its salespeople with as much information as possible so they can serve the customers better.

5. Computer King expects salespeople to keep up with information about the computer industry and the company's competitors.

## LESSON WRAP-UP
*page 93*

Your answers may be something like these:

1. a. I would consider going back to school. I would first talk to my supervisor about seeing if the company would help pay for my continuing education.

b. I would consider talking to my supervisor about why I'm late. I also would consider leaving earlier in the morning or taking a different way across town.

2. Situation: a salesperson trying to get me to buy a car
I would use the skill of drawing conclusions to read information about the car and decide for myself whether this is the right car for me.

## Lesson 13: Working as a Salesclerk

### CHECK YOUR UNDERSTANDING
*page 96*

1. c
2. b
3. a

Your answers may be something like these:

4. If the customer has a complaint, the owner may want to talk to the salesperson. Also, the owner may want to record the number of sales for each salesperson.

5. The customer decided not to take a service contract.

6. No. Customers do not pay tax on the delivery charge. The delivery charge is added after the tax is computed.

### CHECK YOUR UNDERSTANDING
*page 98*

1. c
2. b
3. b
4. A cash register receipt is needed for a refund.
5. No. An employee needs authorization to make a refund.
6. True

7. True
8. False

## LESSON WRAP-UP
*page 99*

Your answers may be something like these:

1. From a medical form on the first visit to a doctor's office, I could conclude that the patient is switching doctors or insurance companies.

2. From an application for citizenship form, I could conclude that the person applying is from another country.

## Lesson 14: Working as a Stock Clerk

### CHECK YOUR UNDERSTANDING
*page 102*

1. b
2. b
3. c
4. False
5. True
6. True
7. The chart describes a process. It gives the steps involved in the process of receiving and checking a shipment.

### CHECK YOUR UNDERSTANDING
*page 104*

1. a
2. b
3. c
4. The equipment may be needed to move stock to the shelves.
5. Turn left, then turn right, and then walk to the back of the stockroom.
6. Your answer may be something like this: Shoes should be organized by size. Manufacturers and colors are likely to vary more than sizes. Also, it would be easier for the salesperson to find shoes for a single customer looking for one or two sizes.

### LESSON WRAP-UP
*page 105*

Your answer may be something like this:
Graphic: a table
To get information from this graphic, I

would use the title and column and row headings to find what I needed.

## UNIT FOUR REVIEW
*page 106*

1. If you know how to draw conclusions, you can get the most information from writing or graphics. You can figure out information that is not stated directly. You can understand a person's point of view and agree or disagree. Finally, you can use your conclusions to make decisions on the job.

2. a. A job application form probably asks for job history, education, military service, and other background information. An employer can tell if you have the background for the job.

b. Tax forms may ask for your name, address, and social security number. They may ask for other information about your tax status. An employer may be able to tell if you are legally eligible for work.

3. a. To show where products are located in a retail store, I would use a floor plan. Floor plans show how things are arranged in a space.

b. To show how a purchase order form goes from the store office to the supplier, I would use a flow chart with boxes and arrows. Flow charts show how a process goes from one stage to the next.

c. To show how a delivery truck gets from the store to a customer's home, I would use a map. A map shows geography. The driver could trace the route along the streets.